Building Value
in Your Company

Howard E. Johnson
MBA, FCA, FCMA, CBV, CPA, CFA, ASA, CF, C.DIR

Disclaimer

The contents of this book are for information and general guidance only. Because the specific facts relating to each company are unique, and because income tax, legal and business situations can change, professional advice should be sought prior to undertaking any significant business initiatives or transactions.

Library and Archives Canada Cataloguing in Publication

Johnson, Howard E.
      Building value in your company / Howard E. Johnson.

ISBN 978-1-55385-586-6

      1. Business enterprises—Valuation.   2. Stockholder wealth. I. Title.

HG4028.V3J64 2011   658.15   C2011-903424-7

© 2011 Howard E. Johnson
Veracap Corporate Finance Limited
70 University Avenue, Suite 320
Toronto, Ontario   M5J 2M4

www.veracap.com

Printed and bound in Canada.

To my loving wife, Julie, and our four wonderful children –

Veronica, Michael, Laura and Russell.

Table of Contents

Table of Exhibits

Preface

Over the past many years, I have had the pleasure and the privilege of being a mergers and acquisitions (M&A) advisor for some of the most astute business owners and executives in the world. Those who built successful companies seemed to understand intuitively what it meant to create shareholder value. They didn't use complicated formulas or a lot of technical jargon. Rather they focused on how to generate cash flow, manage risk and control invested capital when making business decisions. These are the factors that ultimately served to build shareholder value within their company.

While I have written several books on the technical aspects of business valuation, acquisitions and divestitures, I wanted this book to be less formal. This book has been written as if you and I were having a casual conversation about your company over lunch.

I titled this book "Building Value in Your Company" because the process of building value in a company is much like building a house. Creating a strong foundation does not happen overnight. Adequate time and effort are needed to ensure proper planning and construction. However, in the end, a well-built house becomes a lasting legacy.

This book is not intended to make you an expert in business valuation or corporate finance (that's my job!). Rather, it's intended to help you as a business owner or executive to better understand how shareholder value can be:

- **measured** in a realistic and objective manner;
- **created** within your company; and
- **realized** to its maximum potential upon the ultimate sale or succession of your company.

This book does not attempt to give you a precise answer as to how much your company is worth or how to make it worth more. The facts of each specific situation are such that it is not possible to have a magic formula that applies in every case. Rather, this book should be viewed as a general guide, to help you navigate your company in the right direction and to consider the factors that influence shareholder value when making business decisions. While every company is unique, the principles discussed in this book can be broadly applied to virtually any business, be it large or small, public or private.

As a business owner or executive, you should always be running your company as if you were preparing to sell it. While selling your company may be the farthest thing from your current intentions, that philosophy creates a mindset that enforces economic discipline, which in turn helps to build shareholder value. Further, in many cases, the desire or the need to sell arises unexpectedly, such as where an unsolicited offer for your company is received, or where health or other personal reasons emerge. A company that has been run with a disciplined approach to value will help to ensure that shareholder value is maximized, even where the need or the opportunity to sell arises suddenly.

After you have read this book, the three main things that I hope you remember are:

1. Shareholder value is **measured** based on your company's *cash flow* generating capability and its *risk profile*, and these things are interrelated.

2. Shareholder value is **created** by developing a *competitive advantage* that results in earning a return on your invested capital in excess of your cost capital, which in turn generates *intangible value*.

3. Shareholder value is **realized** to its maximum potential by creating liquidity and ensuring that your company's competitive advantage is both *sustainable* and *transferable* to a new owner.

Following along the lines of the above-noted objectives, this book is divided into three parts:

*   Part I deals with value measurement. It addresses various methodologies for determining the value of your company, and the important distinction between tangible net worth and intangible value;

*   Part II deals with value creation. It addresses the importance of developing a competitive advantage through managing your company's cash flow, risk profile and invested capital, which in turn leads to intangible value; and

*   Part III deals with value realization. It addresses the various liquidity alternatives including shareholder distributions, related party transactions and transactions involving third parties.

At the end of each chapter I've highlighted some key points to remember. So sit back, relax and enjoy.

Acknowledgments

I would like to thank Jack Woodcock and Chris Polson for their insightful editorial comments. Thanks also to Elvira Rago and Angela Ingram for their help with various charts and diagrams throughout this book. Finally, a special thanks to Elysia Estee and Dan Bowes for their spirited input.

About the Author

Howard E. Johnson, MBA, FCMA, CA, CBV, CPA, CFA, ASA, CF, C.DIR

Howard is a Managing Director at Veracap Corporate Finance Limited in Toronto, Canada (www.veracap.com), which is a member firm of M&A International, the world's largest affiliation of M&A professionals. Howard helps business owners and executives to maximize shareholder value through acquisitions, divestitures, private equity financing and shareholder value advisory services. He is a frequent speaker at conferences and acts as an expert witness on complex valuation matters before the Courts. Howard has also served as a Director on the Boards of public and private companies.

Howard is the author of *The Acquisition Value Cycle™* (Carswell, 2009), editor of *Corporate Finance for Canadian Executives* (Carswell, 2007), author of *Selling Your Private Company* (Canadian Institute of Chartered Accountants, 2005), co-author of *The Valuation of Business Interests* (Canadian Institute of Chartered Accountants, 2001) and co-editor of *Canada Valuation Service* (Carswell, periodical).

Howard holds a Bachelor of Commerce Degree from Concordia University (Governor General's Award, 1988), a Graduate Diploma in Public Accountancy from McGill University (Kenneth F. Byrd Prize, 1989) and a Masters Degree in Business Administration from McMaster University (D.M. Heddon Gold Medal, 1992). He is a Fellow of the Society of Management Accountants of Canada and holds the designations of Certified Management Accountant, Chartered Accountant, Chartered Business Valuator, Certified Public Accountant, Accredited Senior Appraiser, Corporate Finance Specialist and Chartered Director.

Howard is an avid hockey player. He currently resides in Oakville, Ontario with his wife Julie, and their four children, Veronica, Michael, Laura and Russell.

PART I VALUE MEASUREMENT

BUILDING VALUE IN YOUR COMPANY

1 Principles of Value Measurement

As a starting point, it's important to understand the principles underlying how the value of your company is measured, which is the focus of this chapter. As is the theme with this book, this discussion is not meant to be overly theoretical. However, the principles of value measurement are important to understand so that you can keep them in mind when making business decisions and when interpreting the results of a valuation for your company.

Future Cash Flow is Key

The value of your company is based on its ability to generate cash flow. While accounting earnings are important, there can be many differences between accounting profit and cash flow. Accounting profit is influenced by a myriad of factors, including the accounting policies that your company adopts for such things as inventory costing, depreciation, amortization and leases.

But more specifically, the value of your company is based on the cash flow that it is *expected* to generate in the *future*. So, unlike financial accounting which focuses on measuring historical results, valuation focuses on prospective results. From a valuation standpoint, your company's historical results are only meaningful to the extent that they help in predicting the future.

While there are several different measures of cash flow (which are addressed in Chapter 2), the best measure is *discretionary cash flow,* because it captures all the key elements that influence shareholder value, including cash flow from operations, capital expenditures, income taxes and working capital requirements.

Risk-Reward Trade-Off

Fundamental to valuation is the notion that higher risk should lend itself to higher potential reward. In the financial world, risk is measured in terms of volatility (i.e., the likelihood that actual results will be different from expectations) and the degree of variability. For example, if you have a 50/50 chance of making $10 or losing $10, that proposition is considered less risky than having a 50/50 chance of making $1,000 or losing $1,000. Even though the average expected pay-off is the same, the magnitude of the downside has to be considered in addition to the odds of it happening. Stated another way, given a choice between two possible investments with the same average cash flow expectations, an investor will pay more for the investment with the lower risk profile.

As a practical matter, most business owners and executives are more concerned with down-side risk, rather than pure variability against an average number. Downside risk usually is viewed as the likelihood that the cash flow generated by a company will decline, thereby eroding shareholder value. However, as discussed later in this book, a decline in shareholder value can also result from a higher risk profile or increased capital requirements in order to sustain a company's cash flow.

The lowest risk investment generally is regarded as government bonds. In the economic environment prevailing at the time of writing this book, the yield on long-term government bonds is about 4%. It follows that an investment in a company, which is riskier than govern-ment debt, should command a higher expected rate of return. A large established company might be expected to generate a return on capital of 12% to 15% (after tax), whereas an investment in an early stage business might be expected to generate a return of 25% to 30% or more. Rates of return are discussed in greater detail in Chapter 4. Of course, these are expected rates of return. Only in hindsight will you know whether those expectations were met.

Exhibit 1A : The Risk-Reward Trade-Off

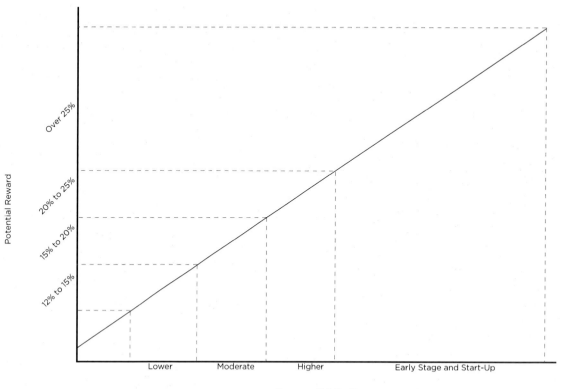

Many business owners struggle with the concept of risk and return when selling their company. For example, let's say that a company generates $10 million of income before taxes and that it could be sold for $50 million. The business owner will often ask, "Why would I sell my company for $50 million when those proceeds will only earn $2 million a year from the yield on government bonds, when I can continue making $10 million a year in profit?" The answer lies in the risk-return profile. An investment in government bonds is a risk-free return, whereas the inherent risk in a single business venture is significantly higher. However, many business owners underestimate the true risk profile of their company.

Enterprise Value vs. Shareholder Value

When we estimate the value of a company, we start by measuring its *enterprise value*, which refers to a company's total value, regardless of how it's financed. Interest bearing debt is deducted from enterprise value to determine *shareholder value* (or equity value), which is the value that accrues to the common shareholders of a company.

Therefore, the key point to remember is that *the enterprise value of your company is independent of how it's financed*. However, shareholder value is affected by the amount of debt financing.

For example, let's say that a snack food manufacturer named Tasty Snacks Ltd. has an enterprise value of $50 million, and it owes the bank $15 million. It follows that the shareholder value of Tasty Snacks is $35 million.

Exhibit 1B : Enterprise Value vs. Shareholder Value, Tasty Snacks Ltd.

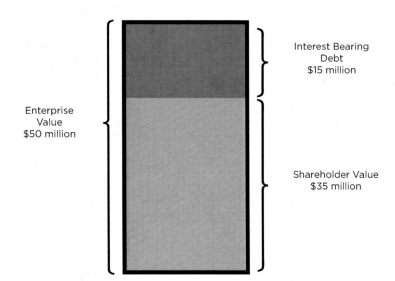

Enterprise
Value
$50 million

Interest Bearing
Debt
$15 million

Shareholder Value
$35 million

This is the same concept as owning a house. If your house is worth $500,000 (aka "enterprise value") and it has a mortgage of $150,000, then the equity value in your house is $350,000 (aka "shareholder value"). The important thing to note here is that the value of your house is independent of how it's financed. So whether you have no mortgage or a large mortgage, your house is still worth $500,000. However, the equity in your house is affected by the amount owing on account of the mortgage. The equity value of your house is what you get to keep after the bank has been paid.

Value is in the Eye of the Beholder

What's the value of your company? It depends on who you ask! Even professional valuators can have significantly different opinions as to the value of a company at a point in time. This is because valuation is a subjective exercise that depends on numerous assumptions. However, we need to distinguish between three different perspectives of value, being:

(i)   value to owner;
(ii) intrinsic value; and
(iii) strategic value.

Many business owners and executives perceive that their company is worth more than it really is. The reason for this is two-fold:

1.   Different perception of risk/return—they are looking at their company from the inside out, which causes them to overstate the strengths and growth prospects of their company, and to understate its weaknesses and risks; and

2.   Commingled concepts of value—they fail to distinguish between the cash flow that their company generates to them as an owner (i.e., *value to owner*) vs. what it would generate if they were not involved in the operations. In many cases, the continued involvement of the business owner is essential in order for a company to prosper. While the business owner may enjoy significant income during the period of their involvement, they may not appreciate the potential consequences relating to over-dependence on them. In such cases, the company is worth more to the current owner than to a buyer. Many business owners get a nasty surprise when they look to sell and discover that their company is not worth what they thought it was, because of its dependence on their continued involvement. Value to owner can also arise from a sentimental attachment to the company.

Intrinsic value refers to the value of your company as a stand-alone entity. This is determined based on the cash flow prospects and risk profile of your company operating on its own. A strategic buyer may offer a premium to the intrinsic value of your company on account of synergies or strategic advantages that would accrue to the buyer through a combination of your company with the buyer's existing operations. This is referred to as *strategic value*. In some cases, the premium for synergies may be significant. However, whether you can get paid a premium on account of synergies when you sell your company rests to a large extent in the structure of the deal and your negotiating abilities. These topics are addressed in subsequent chapters.

Fair Market Value vs. Price

Terms such as *fair market value* and *fair value* often appear in conjunction with an income tax reorganization or corporate law, where shares are being acquired pursuant to a shareholder dispute or related party transaction. When professional valuators determine fair market value, they make certain simplifying assumptions. For example, fair market value assumes that a company is being sold for cash on closing, that neither the buyer nor seller is under compulsion to transact, and that each party has the same knowledge base and equal negotiating capabilities. These assumptions are necessary in order to arrive at a definitive value conclusion.

However, in the open market, some or all of these assumptions do not hold. For example, many transactions are consummated on terms involving forms of consideration other than cash on closing (e.g., promissory notes and earnouts), buyers and sellers sometimes are compelled to transact (e.g., due to health reasons), and the parties to a transaction have a different knowledge base. Inevitably, the seller has the advantage of knowing the details of offers presented to them by various buyers. The buyer has the benefit of knowing the synergies that it will realize following the transaction and its cost of capital, and therefore the maximum price that it can afford to pay (which may be different from its offer).

Therefore, the price paid in an open market transaction may be considerably different (higher or lower) than the fair market value of a company as determined in a notional market context.

Exhibit 1C : Fair Market Value vs. Price

Fair Market Value	Price
An open and unrestricted market exists in which no buyer is excluded	Possible buyers may be excluded due to timing issues, regulatory restrictions, access to financing or other reasons
The buyer and seller have an equal knowledge base	The seller better understands their own business and the options available to them. The buyer better understands the expected synergies and their cost of capital
Neither party is compelled to transact	The seller may need to transact due to health issues or other reasons. The buyer may feel compelled to act in order to maintain the interest of the public equity markets
The transaction is consummated in the form of cash on closing	There can be a variety of different forms of consideration, including holdbacks, promissory notes, share exchanges, earnouts, etc.

The Importance of Liquidity

Liquidity refers to the ability to convert shareholder value into cash. This can be accomplished in a number of ways, ranging from liquidating your company to a third party sale. The opportunity to maximize shareholder value is greatest where there are a large number of prospective buyers or investors in the market and the demand for your company is high. This is a function of prevailing economic and industry conditions, as well as the attractiveness of your company to would-be buyers.

When financing is relatively inexpensive and easily available, it increases the number of potential buyers in the market and the price that they can pay for acquisition targets, thereby increasing the number of transactions and the valuation multiples paid for companies in general. Exhibit 1D illustrates this point. Debt financing was both inexpensive and readily available from around 2005 through to mid-2008. This increased the number of transactions in North America and the median multiple of EBITDA (earnings before interest, taxes, depreciation and amortization) that was paid. When the credit markets tightened in late 2008 and into 2009, the number of transactions and related valuation multiples plummeted. Buyers began to re-enter the market in 2010, which caused valuation multiples to rebound.

Exhibit 1D : # of North American Transactions and Valuation Multiples

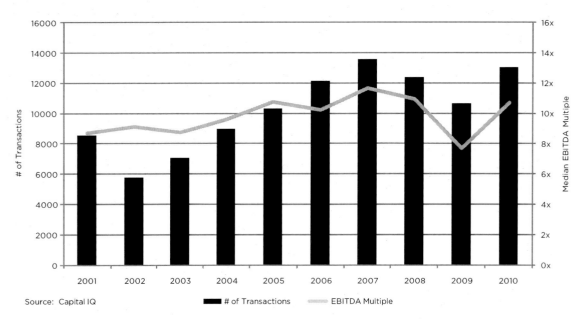

Source: Capital IQ   ■ # of Transactions   ▬ EBITDA Multiple

The liquidity phenomenon is also apparent in the trading prices of shares for publicly held companies. Thinly traded companies often experience an *illiquidity discount*, where there is little interest in the stock, compared to the valuation of widely-held public companies operating in the same industry.

Public Company Values vs. Private Company Values

The value concepts discussed in this book apply to both public and private companies. However, there are important differences between the two types of entities that should be kept in mind. Public companies have added complexities due to formal governance and public disclosure requirements as well as trading restrictions for insiders. Public companies also tend to place a greater emphasis on accounting profit and quarterly financial results. This is because the public equity markets frequently use a price to earnings (P/E) multiple to measure value.

The other major difference is liquidity. The shares of a widely held public company enjoy significant liquidity, which helps to increase their value. This is not the case with privately-held companies. Therefore, within a given industry, it is not uncommon to see the valuation multiples paid for private companies being less than the valuation multiples ascribed to the trading prices of widely held public companies.

As a practical matter, many public companies are reluctant to acquire another company for a multiple that is greater than their prevailing trading multiples in the market for fear of eroding their own price to earnings multiple, and due to the desire to create shareholder value through accretion (i.e., higher earnings per share on a consolidated basis following the transaction).

Controlling Interests vs. Minority Interests

Let's say that the total shareholder value of Tasty Snacks Ltd. is $35 million (i.e., its *en bloc* equity value). It does not necessarily follow that a 10% interest in the shares of Tasty Snacks is worth $3.5 million. Rather, the value of a minority interest can be significantly less than its pro rata amount, particularly in respect of a privately-held company. This is because a minority shareholder in a private company is not in a position to elect a majority of the board of directors and therefore to control the company. Furthermore, a minority interest in a privately-held company may suffer from an *illiquidity discount* given that there generally are fewer buyers interested in acquiring a partial (non-controlling) interest vs. acquiring the company as a whole, and often more restrictions to the transfer of a partial ownership interest.

Discounts for non-control and illiquidity (collectively referred to as a *minority discount*) can vary significantly, from nil to 40% or more from pro rata value. Minority discounts are both subjective and fact-specific. One of the key elements to consider is the provisions of a shareholders' agreement, which establishes the rights, privileges and obligations of both the minority shareholders and the majority shareholders of a company. Shareholders' agreements are discussed in Chapter 11.

Whether or not minority discounts are applicable in the context of a public company is the subject of some debate. However, it is generally accepted that the shares of a widely held public company do not trade with an embedded minority discount. This is because in a widely held public company, no one individual or group has a controlling interest, and because a disenchanted shareholder can readily liquidate their shares if they do not agree with the decisions of the Board of Directors. The advantage of such liquidity typically is not available for minority shareholders of privately-held companies.

Key Points to Remember

- The value of your company is based on the cash flow that it is expected to generate in the future and the risk relating thereto.

- The enterprise value of your company is independent of how it is financed, whereas shareholder value (or equity value) is what you get to keep after the bank has been paid.

- Beware of creating a company that is worth more to the business owner than to a third party buyer.

- Fair market value and price can be dramatically different.

- Greater liquidity results in higher shareholder value.

2 Valuation Based on Multiples

We will start by discussing how companies are valued because you can't tell if you're winning if you don't keep score. Valuation is inherently a subjective exercise. It's based on assumptions and expectations that are subject to change. The key to developing a meaningful valuation conclusion lies in ensuring that the assumptions and expectations used to measure the value of your company are both reasonable and internally consistent.

This chapter presents various approaches to estimating the value of your company by applying a valuation multiple to some measure of its cash flow. The most popular basis is EBITDA (earnings before interest, taxes, depreciation and amortization). Other bases include EBIT (earnings before interest and taxes), EBITDA less capex (i.e., capital expenditures) and after-tax cash flow. In some cases, value is determined based on a multiple of revenues. Remember that the value of your company is based on the cash flow that it is expected to generate in the future and the risk related thereto. Therefore, measures such as historical EBITDA or EBIT should be considered as only a proxy for future cash flow.

While the multiple of EBITDA methodology and similar approaches are popular due to their simplicity, they are fraught with challenges and can even generate misleading results. It follows that these valuation approaches should be applied with caution. They are often useful as a preliminary indication of value, or as a test of the results determined pursuant to another methodology, such as discounted cash flow (discussed in the next chapter).

Revenue Multiples

The value of your company might be expressed as a multiple of its historical or current (e.g., past 12 months or current year forecast) revenues. While revenues may be far removed from profit or cash flow, this methodology sometimes is used to draw a broad indication as to value. The mechanics of the multiple of revenue methodology are as follows:

Exhibit 2A : Multiple of Revenue Methodology

	Revenue Base
Multiplied by:	Revenue Multiple
Equals:	Enterprise Value
Deduct:	Interest Bearing Debt Outstanding
Equals:	Shareholder Value

A multiple of revenue approach sometimes is used when assessing the value of an early stage company or one that is experiencing operating losses (or is not yet generating normalized levels of cash flow). The assumption is that over the longer term the company will generate positive cash flow and represent a going concern. However, this is not always the case.

The value of technology companies sometimes is referenced in terms of a multiple of revenue. For example, at the time of writing, it is not unusual for software company valuations to fall in the range of 1x to 3x revenue. Exactly where a company falls within this range (or outside of the range) depends on numerous factors, including the nature of its revenues (e.g., recurring vs. non-recurring) and growth prospects related thereto.

While attractive due to its simplicity, the multiple of revenue approach has significant shortcomings. First and foremost, higher revenues do not necessarily translate into higher shareholder value (or even higher cash flow). Second, revenue multiples are based on broad generalizations that may not hold in a specific set of circumstances. It follows that the multiple of revenue methodology may be useful as a preliminary indication of value or as a test of valuation conclusions derived pursuant to other methodologies, but seldom is valid as a primary approach. That being said, in many cases, reported industry transactions only provide sufficient information to determine the multiple of revenue that was paid. Therefore, the multiple of revenue methodology may have some use as a comparator against industry transactions.

Cash Flow Multiples

The mathematics of valuations based on cash flow multiples is relatively straightforward. A valuation multiple is applied to the cash flow base to determine the *enterprise value* of your company. Recall that enterprise value represents the total operating value of your company, regardless of how it's financed. Outstanding interest-bearing debt is then deducted to determine shareholder value.

Since the level of debt within your company is readily discernable, it follows that the key variables to consider are: (i) the cash flow base; and (ii) the valuation multiple applied thereto.

The Multiple of EBITDA Methodology

The multiple of EBITDA (earnings before interest, taxes, depreciation and amortization) methodology is one of the most popular approaches to business valuation. In open market transactions, buyers and sellers often refer to a multiple of EBITDA when negotiating a deal.

EBITDA reflects your company's operating cash flow, before consideration of financing, income taxes or capital expenditure requirements. In its basic form, the multiple of EBITDA methodology is as follows:

Exhibit 2B : Multiple of EBITDA Methodology

	Normalized EBITDA
Multiplied by:	EBITDA Multiple
Equals:	Enterprise Value
Deduct:	Interest Bearing Debt Outstanding
Equals:	Shareholder Value

Note that the starting point is *normalized* EBITDA, which is typically based on your company's historical or current operating results. Since valuation is future-oriented, we have to adjust historical or current results to remove the impact of discretionary expenditures, as well as unusual and non-recurring revenues and expenses that are not expected to be incurred in the future. Normalization adjustments are discussed in the next section.

The EBITDA multiple reflects the risk that EBITDA will not be maintained at the indicated normalized level, as well as the prospects for future growth. We'll discuss the factors that drive valuation multiples later in this chapter.

Despite its popularity, the multiple of EBITDA methodology has serious limitations. Most notably, the EBITDA base ignores capital expenditure requirements and income taxes, which must somehow be reflected in the valuation multiple. Furthermore, depending on the accounting standards that your company adopts, certain costs may be capitalized and amortized over a period of time, rather than being expensed in the period they are incurred (e.g., product development costs). Where such expenditures are not somehow accounted for in the multiple of EBITDA methodology, the resultant value conclusion can be distorted.

As a result, sophisticated investors usually adopt more comprehensive valuation models (such as the discounted cash flow methodology, discussed in the next chapter) when estimating the value of a company. However, investors often will convert the valuation results derived pursuant to those more sophisticated methodologies into a multiple of EBITDA equivalent when referring to value or when negotiating the purchase or sale of a company.

The Multiple of EBIT Methodology

The Multiple of EBIT (earnings before interest and taxes) methodology attempts to compensate for one of the major deficiencies in the Multiple of EBITDA methodology – ignoring capital spending. The multiple of EBIT methodology is as follows:

Exhibit 2C : Multiple of EBIT Methodology

	Normalized EBITDA
Deduct:	Depreciation and Amortization
Equals:	Normalized EBIT
Multiplied by:	EBIT Multiple
Equals:	Enterprise Value
Deduct:	Interest Bearing Debt Outstanding
Equals:	Shareholder Value

EBIT sometimes is used as a proxy for cash flow before income taxes and financing. Its validity as a cash flow proxy depends on whether depreciation and amortization expense for accounting purposes approximates your company's sustaining capital expenditure requirements. If so, then normalized EBIT has some merit as a cash flow proxy (before tax).

Since capital expenditure requirements are reflected in the EBIT base, the EBIT multiple does not have to account for that factor. Therefore, your company's EBIT multiple is higher than its EBITDA multiple.

The Multiple of EBITDA Less Capex Methodology

The Multiple of EBITDA less Capex methodology also explicitly considers capital expenditure (i.e., "capex") requirements. It is preferable to the Multiple of EBIT methodology where ongoing capital expenditure requirements do not reflect historical depreciation and amortization expense for accounting purposes. This is particularly the case for companies that operate in capital intensive industries.

Exhibit 2D : Multiple of EBITDA Less Capex Methodology

	Normalized EBITDA
Deduct:	Sustaining Capital Expenditures
Equals:	Normalized EBITDA Less Capex
Multiplied by:	EBITDA Less Capex Multiple
Equals:	Enterprise Value
Deduct:	Interest Bearing Debt Outstanding
Equals:	Shareholder Value

Sustaining capital expenditures should reflect the average annual capital spending required in order to maintain your company's normalized EBITDA at the level indicated. This may or may not be different than depreciation and amortization expense for accounting purposes.

Sustaining capital expenditures may also be quite different from actual capital spending in a given year. In many cases, a company's capital expenditure requirements are "lumpy", as major spending initiatives take place in some years and not others. The sustaining capital expenditure estimate deducted in this methodology should reflect a long-term average amount in order to maintain the indicated EBITDA. A thorough analysis of capital spending requirements necessitates an objective assessment of the nature and condition of your company's fixed assets and its capital needs over the longer term.

Multiple of After-Tax Cash Flow

The Multiple of After-Tax Cash Flow methodology considers both capital spending requirements and income taxes. The basic methodology is as follows:

PART I • VALUE MEASUREMENT

Exhibit 2E : Multiple of After-Tax Cash Flow Methodology

	Normalized EBITDA
Deduct:	Depreciation and Amortization
Equals:	Normalized EBIT
Deduct:	Cash Income Taxes
Equals:	Normalized After-Tax Income
Add:	Depreciation and Amortization
Deduct:	Sustaining Capital Expenditures
Equals:	Normalized After-Tax Cash Flow
Multiplied by:	After-Tax Cash Flow Multiple
Equals:	Enterprise Value
Deduct:	Interest Bearing Debt Outstanding
Equals:	Shareholder Value

Depreciation and amortization are deducted from normalized EBITDA to calculate normalized EBIT. The implicit assumption is that depreciation and amortization for accounting purposes approximates allowable depreciation for tax purposes. Cash income taxes are deducted based on the applicable income tax rate. The cash taxes calculation takes into account the timing of when revenues and expenses are recognized for income tax purposes. Therefore, cash income taxes may be different than income taxes for accounting purposes, which is based on accounting income rather than taxable income.

Since depreciation and amortization are a non-cash expense, they are then added back. Sustaining capital expenditures are deducted in order to calculate normalized after-tax cash flow. Depending on the nature of your company, sustaining capital expenditures may or may not approximate depreciation and amortization expense.

The after-tax cash flow multiple should reflect the fact that capital expenditures and income taxes have been taken into account. Therefore, the after-tax cash flow multiple applicable to your company will be higher than other multiples based on EBITDA, EBIT or EBITDA less capex.

Calculating Normalized EBITDA

The starting point for the cash flow-based valuation methodologies presented in this chapter is normalized EBITDA. Recall from Chapter 1 that the value of your company is based on the cash flow that it is expected to generate in the future. Therefore, historical and current

14   BUILDING VALUE IN YOUR COMPANY

operating results may have to be adjusted to account for discretionary spending, as well as unusual and non-recurring revenues and expenses that are not expected to occur in the future. Making normalization adjustments can be a subjective exercise.

The first question that usually gets asked is, "How many years of historical operating results should I look at when calculating normalized EBITDA?" Well, it depends. *Historical and current operating results are only meaningful to the extent that they reflect future expectations.* Consider the following:

- if your company operates in a cyclical industry, it may be appropriate to consider the average operating results over an economic cycle, rather than applying the valuation multiple to a high point or low point in the cycle;

- if your company underwent significant changes to its operations a few years ago (e.g., bought or sold a division, entered into a new market or experienced major changes in its product line), then the operating results prior to those changes may not be reflective of future results; and

- if your company has grown significantly over the past few years, then its most recent operating results or current year forecast may be the best indicator of what is to come.

Once you have determined which historical and current operating results are most relevant, then for each selected year, you can make the following calculation.

Exhibit 2F : Normalized EBITDA Calculation

	Income Before Taxes as Reported
Add:	Interest Expense
Equals:	Actual EBIT
Add (deduct):	Normalization Adjustments
Equals:	Normalized EBIT
Add:	Depreciation and Amortization Expense
Equals:	Normalized EBITDA

The starting point in determining normalized EBITDA is your company's historical or current income statement. Income before taxes represents the pre-tax profit that your company generated for accounting purposes. As discussed in Chapter 1, there are numerous reasons that accounting profit may be different from cash flow. Note that we start with pre-tax income (instead of after-tax) because the income taxes that are deducted against normalized income may be considerably different than the income tax expense as shown on your company's income statement.

Interest expense is then added back. Why? Because, as noted in Chapter 1, the enterprise value of your company is independent of how it's financed. Financing does impact shareholder value, by way of deducting interest-bearing debt outstanding from enterprise value. Therefore, in the first instance, we want to set aside financing and deal with the operating value (i.e., enterprise value) of your company. The result of adding interest expense to pretax income is actual EBIT (i.e., earnings before interest and taxes).

Actual EBIT is then adjusted for the following normalization adjustments, where applicable:

- Remuneration to your company's shareholders and related parties. In privately-held companies it's common for the shareholders to pay salaries, bonuses and other remuneration to themselves and related parties at levels that do not reflect market rates. This is often done for income tax purposes. Therefore, remuneration paid to the shareholders and related parties in your company should be added back to income. However, in determining normalized EBITDA, it's important to deduct market rate salaries for those individuals based on the role that they actually perform. For non-active individuals this is nil. However, for an active shareholder that fills the role of President or other executive, the market rate remuneration to replace that person (including salaries, bonuses and benefits) could be significant. *Fundamental to the determination of shareholder value is the segregation of return on labour from return on capital.* Shareholders of privately-held companies must pay themselves first, based on market rates for the role that they are fulfilling. Cash flow that remains within your company after the active shareholders have been paid market-based salaries represents a return on capital;

- Rental payments. In some cases, a company's operations are situated in facilities that are owned by the company or related parties. As further discussed in Chapter 5, real estate should be viewed as a separate asset from the business because of its different (usually lower) risk profile. Therefore, if your company owns its land and building, normalized EBITDA should be reduced on account of a market-based rent for the property. This adjustment effectively reduces the value of your company's operations, but reallocates that value (or more – see Chapter 5) to the real estate component. Similarly, if the property is held by a related party, an adjustment to reported EBITDA may be necessary to reflect market rental rates, as opposed to what was actually paid;

- Discretionary expenses. In some cases (more often in privately-held companies), shareholders incur corporate expenses that are not required as part of its operations (such as personal expenses). To the extent that you can identify discretionary expenses in your company, they should be added back to historical income, on the basis that they really reflect a return on capital as opposed to an economic cost (much like remuneration levels that are above market rates). However, you need to be satisfied that those expenses are truly discretionary, and that their discontinuance would not impair your company's operations or risk profile over the longer term;

- Unusual or non-recurring items. To the extent that your company incurred expenses or generated income in the past that are of an unusual or non-recurring nature, that expense (income) should be added back (deducted) on the basis that it is not expected to occur in the future. In this regard, you need to ensure that these items are truly unusual and non-recurring, as opposed to expenses (or income) that may be incurred once every few years, and which therefore should be factored into normalized EBITDA; and

• Income and expenses relating to *redundant assets*. As discussed in Chapter 5, redundant assets are those that are not required in the ongoing operations of your company (e.g., vacant land). Redundant assets are considered as a separate component of value. Accordingly, any income or expenses attributed to those redundant assets should be removed from historical results so as to avoid double-counting.

Adjusting historical EBIT for normalizing items results in "normalized EBIT".

When depreciation and amortization (being non-cash charges) are added back to normalized EBIT, the result is "normalized EBITDA" (earnings before interest, taxes, depreciation and amortization).

What Are Valuation Multiples?

A valuation multiple is the inverse of a rate of return on capital. For example, if the rate of return is 20%, the equivalent valuation multiple would be calculated as: 1/20% = 5x

Valuation multiples inherently are subjective. No one in the world can say what the "right" multiple is for a particular company. That's why company values normally are expressed within a range. Regardless of how they may be expressed, when determining valuation multiples, it's important to be internally consistent. That is to say, *the basis of determining the valuation multiple must be consistent with the cash flow base against which it is being applied*. Therefore, after-tax multiples have to be applied to after-tax cash flows, and pre-tax multiples (e.g., multiples of EBIT and EBITDA) must be applied to those respective pre-tax measures.

Consider the example of Tasty Snacks Ltd. The company generates $10 million in normalized EBITDA on $100 million in revenues. Tasty Snacks has recorded $2.85 million of depreciation and amortization expense (which approximates sustaining capital requirements), and pays cash income taxes at a rate of 30%. If a reasonable estimate of the enterprise value of Tasty Snacks is $50 million, that figure can be derived through a multiple of 0.5x revenues, 5x EBITDA, 7x EBIT or 10x after-tax cash flow.

Exhibit 2G : Tasty Snacks Ltd.—Internal Consistency in Valuation Multiples $(000)

	Cash Flow	Valuation Multiple	Rate of Return
Revenues	100,000	0.5x	n/a
Operating Expenses	90,000		
Normalized EBITDA	10,000	5.0x	20%
Depreciation (Capex)	2,850		
Normalized EBIT	7,150	7.0x	14%
Income Taxes	2,150		
After-Tax Cash Flow	5,000	10.0x	10%

All results lead to a $50 million enterprise value.

It's astonishing how often someone will refer to a valuation multiple without knowing whether it's a multiple of EBITDA, EBIT or after-tax cash flow. This makes the valuation multiple meaningless. What's worse, by commingling multiples and cash flow definitions, the resultant value conclusion is misleading. To reinforce the point – *the cash flow base and the valuation multiple applied thereto are interrelated, and each cannot be assessed in isolation.*

Factors Influencing Valuation Multiples

There are numerous factors that can influence valuation multiples in any fact-specific situation. Valuation multiples reflect the expectations as to future cash flow, given your company's risk profile and growth prospects. Valuation multiples are also influenced by comparable transactions and public equity market multiples.

Competitive Advantage

Companies that have developed some uniqueness or competitive advantage in their product or service offerings enjoy higher valuation multiples. This may come in the form of proprietary technology, an established brand name or other advantages which are difficult for competitors to easily replicate (i.e., "barriers to entry"). A competitive advantage in your company's product or service offerings also makes it difficult for customers to leave (i.e., "barriers to exit").

A competitive advantage can also be attributable to such things as a strong distribution network, strategic location, proprietary production equipment or other factors that help to differentiate your company and to generate superior economic returns vs. your competitors. However, your competitive advantage must be *sustainable* and *transferable* in order to translate into a higher valuation multiple for your company. I'll discuss these concepts in Chapter 6.

Revenue Stability and Diversification

Your company's customer base has a significant impact on its value. Valuation multiples are higher for companies that have a diverse base of repeat customers as opposed to companies that are dependent on a handful of customers or have little in the way of repeat business. In particular, companies that have developed a "sticky" customer base, meaning that the likelihood that customers will remain loyal to the company is high (also referred to as "barriers to exit") enjoy a premium multiple. Customer stickiness extends from your company's competitive advantage, as noted above.

Management Team

For most companies, the management and employees are one of its most important assets, if not *the* most important. In some cases, employees may have specialized skills or knowledge that may be difficult to replace. Skilled employees can create a barrier to entry for competitors or be an attractive asset for a strategic buyer, thereby increasing the valuation multiple.

Likewise, the breadth and depth of your company's management team can significantly impact its valuation multiple. Where a good management succession plan is not in place, the valuation multiple may suffer. In cases where the business owner and family members are actively involved in a company, that factor can have negative implications on the company's risk profile if strong successors cannot be readily identified.

Supply Risk

Companies are subject to supply risk where they are exposed to supplier concentration, or key raw materials may not otherwise be available due to general market shortages. Supply risk can also stem from fluctuating raw materials prices, which is common in many commodities.

Supply risk should not be viewed solely from the standpoint of raw materials. Rather, it should encompass all of the inputs required to operate your company, including utilities, machinery, spare parts and other requirements. Shortages in labour supply would also fall into this category.

Competitive Landscape

The nature and extent of competition within an industry will impact the valuation multiple. Where competition is intense and driven toward price, the valuation multiple tends to be lower. Companies operating in an industry characterized by large, well-financed competitors may be subject to a lower valuation multiple if they are unable to effectively compete against those Goliaths. Conversely, a fragmented industry may be viewed as opportunistic, if your company can distinguish itself within a particular niche.

Company Size

In many cases, smaller companies within a given industry fetch lower valuation multiples than their larger counterparts. This is particularly the case where a small company has a limited market presence and is reliant on a handful of customers or employees. As a practical matter, in open market transactions, smaller companies usually generate less interest among buyers thereby reducing liquidity and hence value (i.e., an *illiquidity discount*). If these factors are already reflected in the valuation multiple, then it is important not to double-count their impact.

That being said, some smaller companies experience less of a discount than others. In particular, if a company regardless of size, represents an important strategic opportunity for a buyer, then the buyer may pay a price that is representative of *strategic value*, which is reflected in the valuation multiple. This sometimes happens with technology companies that have proprietary software or other technical aspects in their product offering that the buyer can leverage.

Growth Expectations

Companies with a demonstrated history of growth (in terms of revenues and cash flow) and the prospect that such growth will continue will usually fetch higher valuation multiples. This is because valuation is forward-looking, and value is driven by future cash flow. By way of example, if the EBITDA for Tasty Snacks is expected to grow by 10% in the coming year, from $10 million to $11 million, then a multiple of 5x historical EBITDA translates into a multiple of 4.5x forward EBITDA.

Exhibit 2H : Valuation Multiples and Growth

	This Year	Next Year
Normalized EBITDA	$10 million	$11 million
EBITDA Multiple	5x	4.5x
Enterprise Value	$50 million	$50 million (rounded)

One of the challenges with factoring a growth element into the valuation multiple is that there are other factors that influence shareholder value. For example, growing companies often require additional capital spending and working capital in order to accommodate growth. Therefore, any adjustment to the cash flow multiple on account of growth must take the cost of growth into account.

Capital Expenditure Requirements

When applying a multiple of revenue or multiple of EBITDA methodology, the valuation multiple must take into account your company's capital expenditure requirements, since capital spending is not reflected in these cash flow proxies. Companies with low capital expenditure requirements tend to fetch higher valuation multiples. This is because a greater proportion of revenues or EBITDA, as the case may be, will fall to the bottom line, rather than having to be re-invested into the company in order to maintain its operations.

Debt Capacity

The greater the ability of your company to finance its operations with debt rather than equity, the higher its valuation multiple. This is because the cost of debt financing is lower than equity financing, and the use of debt serves to reduce the cost of capital. Your company's debt capacity is influenced by the level and stability of its cash flow (required to service interest and principal repayments) and the amount and quality of its underlying assets. There is further discussion about cost of capital in Chapter 4.

Industry, Economic and Capital Market Conditions

Industry and economic conditions also influence valuation multiples. Many industries go through cycles. Where the industry in which your company operates is undergoing a period of consolidation, valuation multiples tend to be higher than would otherwise be the case because of the number of buyers actively seeking acquisition targets (i.e., greater liquidity). In addition, valuation multiples are higher in buoyant economic times than in more depressed economic times. Where the capital markets are such that debt and equity financing is readily available on attractive terms, that factor spurs buying activity, which in turn increases valuation multiples.

Industry Transactions

Valuation multiples are influenced by transactions involving other companies in your industry. However, comparable transaction multiples often are not publicly disclosed, particularly where both the buyer and seller are privately-held companies. Even where they are disclosed, you won't know the relative negotiating position of the buyer and seller, the perceived synergies or other important factors, all of which may have affected the stated purchase price and implied valuation multiple. Further, there may be limited or incomplete disclosure of important elements of the transaction, such as the terms of payment, which may also have a significant impact on the reported valuation multiple. Valuation multiples tend to be lower where the terms of payment are cash on closing, as opposed to where some of the purchase price is paid over time, or is contingent upon the prospective operating results of the acquired company.

In some cases, industry transaction multiples can be misleading. This is because multiples are calculated based on *reported* results, as opposed to *normalized* earnings, which generally are not known outside of those directly involved in the transaction. For example, if a company was acquired for $50 million based on reported EBITDA of $7 million, it would suggest that a multiple of about 7x EBITDA was paid for that company. However, it may be the case that the target company had $3 million of non-recurring expenses that, when adjusted for, resulted in normalized EBITDA of $10 million, and a "true" multiple of 5x EBITDA. However, this fact would not be known to a third party observer.

Despite the caveats associated with over-reliance on industry transaction multiples, you should keep apprised of the transactions going on within your industry. The reason for this is two-fold. First, it can have obvious ramifications on the competitive landscape within your industry and consequently impact the risk profile of your company. Second, you may recall the underlying principle that greater liquidity leads to higher value. Therefore, even if the prices and multiples associated with industry transactions cannot be deciphered based on the information disclosed, the number of transactions within your industry provides an indication of market interest, which influences liquidity and by extension, the valuation multiple.

Public Equity Market Multiples

The valuation multiples for your company are also influenced by public equity market multiples of companies operating within your industry. If you operate a public company, you likely will have seen analyst reports that compare the valuation multiple of your company against its peers. If your company is private, you need to consider the fundamental differences between public equity market multiples and those that can be applied to the valuation of a private company (as discussed in Chapter 1), or even to a public company pursuant to a takeover bid. Furthermore, in the case of both industry transactions and public market multiples, you need to consider differences between any two companies, in terms of product and service offerings, markets served, customer base and other variables. These things can result in significantly different multiples for companies that may appear to be similar.

As discussed in Chapter 1, it's not uncommon for private companies to be valued at a multiple that is below publicly-held comparables due to differences in liquidity. While applying public equity market multiples to a privately-held company usually is not appropriate, public equity market multiples may provide some general guidance with respect to relative magnitude and overall trends. Public equity market multiples may be more meaningful for large private companies where an initial public offering is a viable option to a sale, or where the company being valued is public itself.

Exhibit 2I : Factors Influencing Valuation Multiples

- Competitive advantage

- Revenue stability and diversification

- Management team

- Supplier risk

- Competitive landscape

- Company size

- Growth expectations

- Capital expenditure requirements

- Debt capacity

- Industry, economic and credit market conditions

- Industry transactions

- Public equity market multiples

General Ranges for Valuation Multiples

Valuation multiples are influenced by a range of factors that can cause them to vary widely, even among companies within the same industry. As noted above, larger, more established companies tend to fetch higher valuation multiples than smaller companies, because larger companies tend to be more diversified in terms of customers, markets served and so on. Further, a company's growth prospects also have a major influence on valuation multiples because valuation is forward-looking. Based on these two parameters, as a very general guideline at the time of writing, it is not unusual to see multiples of normalized EBITDA fall within the following ranges for privately-held companies:

Exhibit 2J : General Ranges of Valuation Multiples

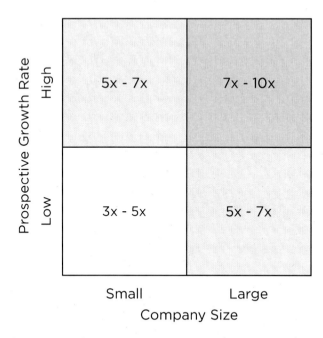

Multiples in excess of 10x normalized EBITDA sometimes are paid for highly desirable companies operating in high-growth industries and offering significant synergies to a strategic buyer. Such multiples are also highly dependent on the negotiating position of the seller and the structure of the deal, which are discussed in subsequent chapters.

The multiples shown in Exhibit 2K are generally lower than the median EBITDA multiples for publicly-traded companies as noted earlier in this chapter. Public companies tend to be larger than private companies, and there are differences in liquidity between the trading prices of shares in the public market vs. the prices of privately-held companies viewed *en bloc*.

Interest Bearing Debt and Cash

As noted in all of the valuation methodologies, outstanding interest-bearing debt is deducted from enterprise value to determine your company's shareholder value. Interest-bearing debt includes both short-term debt and long-term debt, such as operating loans, term loans, capital lease obligations, etc. It also includes equivalent obligations, such as advances from shareholders and related parties, whether or not they bear interest. This is because such obligations would have to be settled if your company were sold.

Interest-bearing debt does not include operating liabilities such as accounts payable, accrued liabilities, deferred revenues, warranties and similar liabilities. While such debts have to be settled as well, they provide an ongoing source of trade financing for your company in the ordinary course of business.

If your company has cash on its books, then that cash normally offsets interest-bearing debt outstanding, or is otherwise added to shareholder value, subject to the need for adequate working capital levels to support your company's operations. Debt financing and working capital are further discussed in Chapter 4.

Adjustments to the Shareholder Value Conclusion

In some cases, further adjustments are needed to your company's shareholder value as otherwise determined pursuant to one of the methodologies presented in this chapter. Applying a valuation multiple to a cash flow base inherently assumes those cash flows will remain relatively stable or increase at a constant rate over the long term. However, in some cases, a company may expect to incur a one-time cost or benefit in the near term. Examples include income from a one-time gain (e.g., the pending receipt of insurance proceeds) or non-recurring operating expenses (e.g., the cost to clean up contaminated land). Where prospective revenues or expenses are non-recurring, they are not multiplied by a valuation multiple. Rather, their impact (net of taxes) should be reflected through a one-time addition to (or deduction from) shareholder value otherwise determined.

Adjustments to shareholder value may also be made on account of excess or deficient working capital or where real estate exists within your company. These adjustments are discussed in Chapter 5.

Key Points to Remember

- While estimating the value of your company based on a multiple of EBITDA methodology may be popular, you have to keep in mind the limitations of that approach.

- Historical operating results are only meaningful to the extent that they help in predicting the future.

- You need to distinguish between *return on labour* and *return on capital*.

- There must be internal consistency between the determination of the valuation multiple and the cash flow base against which it is applied.

- You can increase your company's valuation multiple by developing a sustainable and transferable competitive advantage, a diverse base of repeat customers, and a strong management team.

3 Valuation Based on Discounted Cash Flows

The discounted cash flow (DCF) methodology generally is the preferred basis of valuation. Sophisticated investors normally adopt the DCF methodology as their primary valuation approach and then supplement their value conclusions with other methodologies such as the Multiple of EBITDA as a test for reasonableness.

In this chapter, we will discuss the mechanics of the DCF methodology and how its components are determined. As I said at the outset of this book, I am not trying to turn you into a valuation expert. Rather, you should look at the DCF methodology as a management tool. When properly developed, the DCF methodology can provide great insights into how shareholder value can be created within your company. This is because it will force you to explicitly consider all of the major variables that ultimately impact shareholder value and how business decisions impact those variables.

It's worth the time and effort to develop a DCF model that takes a comprehensive look at all of the major business inputs and lends itself to sensitivity analysis. Once developed, the model should be relatively easy to use and to update.

If you run a privately-held company, as a matter of good business practice, you should conduct an annual DCF-based valuation. For most business owners, their company is their biggest investment, so it's important to have a good sense as to what the company is worth, and whether or not its value is increasing or decreasing over time.

The value of a public company is readily discernable from the trading price of the shares. However, it still makes sense to compare a DCF-based internal valuation to the market price. That exercise can help in gauging market expectations and in assessing the possible reasons for the discrepancy between internally based values and public market values.

Mechanics of the DCF Methodology

The mechanics of the DCF methodology can be complicated. However, in its basic form, the DCF methodology consists of six steps.

1. A forecast is made of the *discretionary cash flow* that your company is expected to generate in each of the next few years (generally three to five years).

2. The discretionary cash flow for each year of the forecast period is discounted to a present value amount using a *discount rate*.

3. The *terminal value* is calculated by estimating the annual maintainable discretionary cash flow beyond the forecast period, divided by a *capitalization rate*. The terminal value represents the estimated enterprise value of your company beyond the forecast period.

4. The terminal value amount is discounted to its present value amount using the discount rate applied to the annual discretionary cash flows.

5. The present value of the forecast discretionary cash flows and the present value of the terminal value are added together to determine the enterprise value of your company.

6. Outstanding interest-bearing debt is deducted from enterprise value to derive the shareholder value of your company.

Therefore, the key components of the DCF methodology are:
   (i)   the forecast discretionary cash flow;
   (ii) the discount rate; and
   (iii) the terminal value.

A graphical illustration of the components of the DCF methodology is set out in Exhibit 3A.

Exhibit 3A : Graphical Depiction of the Discounted Cash Flow Methodology

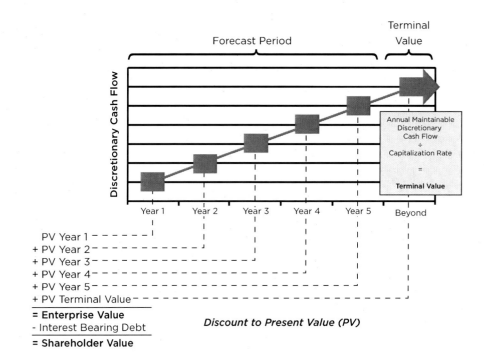

Forecast Discretionary Cash Flow

Discretionary cash flow represents the cash that is available as a return on total capital after all costs of doing business have been taken into account. Discretionary cash flow captures all of the operating cash components of your company (excluding interest expense, which is a financing cost). In its simplified form, discretionary cash flow is calculated as follows:

Exhibit 3B : Calculation of Discretionary Cash Flow

	EBIT (Earnings Before Interest and Taxes)
Deduct:	Cash Income Taxes
Equals:	After-Tax Income Before Financing
Add:	Depreciation and Amortization
Deduct:	Sustaining and Growth Capital Expenditure Requirements
Deduct:	Incremental Working Capital Required to Support Growth
Equals:	Discretionary Cash Flow

In comparing discretionary cash flow used in the DCF methodology (as determined above) to after-tax cash flow as shown in Chapter 2, there are three important things to note:

1. There is no need for normalization adjustments in the DCF methodology, since we are dealing with future cash flows, as opposed to historical or current results.

2. Capital expenditure requirements in the DCF methodology reflect not only sustaining capital, but also growth capital. In this regard, companies often have to incur additional capital expenditures in order to accommodate growth. This can also increase the amount of sustaining capital required over the longer term. *There must be internal consistency between the forecast operating cash flows and the capital expenditures required to support those results.*

3. Incremental working capital is factored into the DCF methodology. As a company grows, it usually requires more working capital (i.e., accounts receivable, inventory, etc.) in order to support that growth. This is an important consideration that's often overlooked. Working capital represents after-tax dollars that must be reinvested in your company. The drain on cash flow caused by incremental working capital can significantly reduce shareholder value.

The validity of the value conclusion derived pursuant to the DCF methodology is dependent upon the quality of the forecast and discount rate assumptions. It's a case of "garbage in, garbage out". As a general rule, those preparing forecasts tend to be overly optimistic. Most business owners and executives like to believe that their company will grow – sometimes quite rapidly. They often look through rose-coloured glasses.

Most forecasts are prepared for a period of three to five years. A common reaction among business owners and executives is that they have no idea what will happen five months from now, let alone five years. The one thing that is true about forecasts is that they are always wrong! However, the purpose of forecasting is not to create an exact picture of the future, but rather to develop a plausible scenario of the longer term financial results for your company. The forecasting exercise should help you to consider what resources (e.g., working capital, employees, capital spending, etc.) will be required in order to achieve forecast operating results.

The DCF model should be developed in a way that makes it easy to change key assumptions and to conduct sensitivity analysis. This can help you to better understand the degree of risk inherent in your company and the impact on the value conclusions by changing a few variables. The greater the sensitivity of the valuation conclusion to changes in assumptions, the greater the risk profile of your company.

The forecast should incorporate certain reasonableness tests, such as capacity utilization, operating costs as a percentage of revenues, working capital as a percentage of revenues, implied market share, revenues per employee and other metrics. This will help you to avoid getting carried away with growth assumptions that result in an unrealistic value conclusion. A common error that people make in forecasts is to assume that revenues will grow much faster than expenses, thereby increasing profit margins over time. As discussed in Chapter 7, companies often incur *step costs* as they become larger, which can significantly impact value.

Having an adequate level of detail will also help to establish credibility in a forecast. While it's difficult to forecast revenues by customer, by product or service offering, etc., doing so will help you to explicitly consider where growth likely can be generated, which by extension forces you to consider how that might be achieved. For example, you should think about what percentage of growth will be derived from existing products as opposed to new products, and the extent to which that growth will come from existing customers vs. new customers.

The more time and effort expended on preparing a forecast, the more useful the forecasting exercise. The forecast should contain a complete set of projected financial statements (income statement, balance sheet and cash flow statement) as that will help to ensure that all of the key variables have been considered. Your accountant can help you with the mechanics of compiling the forecast, but they will need your input in order to develop meaningful forecasting scenarios and assumptions.

Discount Rates

Applying a discount rate to forecast discretionary cash flows (i.e., determining the present value of forecast discretionary cash flows) is based on the underlying principle that a dollar received at some point in the future is worth less than a dollar received today. The relative worth of a dollar received in the future is based on two factors, being:

1. How many years into the future the dollar will be received; and

2. The discount rate applied thereto.

As illustrated in Exhibit 3C, a dollar received many years into the future, or which is subject to a high discount rate, is worth considerably less than a dollar received today.

Exhibit 3C : Present Value of $1 Received in the Future

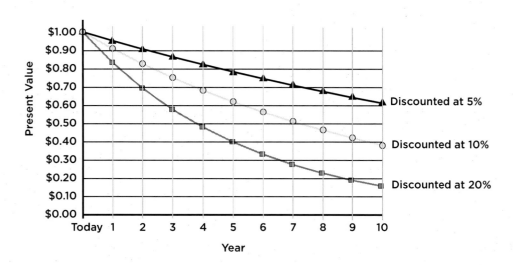

The formula for determining the present value factor for $1.00 received at some point in the future is as follows:

Present value factor = $1.00 / (1 + discount rate) $^{\text{number of years in the future}}$

For example, the present value factor given a rate of return of 15% for $1.00 received at the end of 3 years would be determined as:

$$\$1.00 / (1 + .15)^3 = 0.658$$

It follows that $1 received 3 years from now at a 15% discount rate is worth about $0.66.

In the context of the DCF methodology, the discount rate is expressed as a *weighted average cost of capital* (WACC). The WACC is an *after-tax* rate of return based on what is considered to be a *normalized* mix of debt and equity to finance your company, regardless of the extent to which debt financing is actually used. This is because the enterprise value of your company is independent of how it's financed. The WACC discount rate is applied to discretionary cash flows, before financing costs (i.e., interest expense and principal repayments) as calculated in the previous section.

While discount rates are subjective, it's not unusual to see nominal (i.e., including inflation) WACC discount rates in the range of 10% to 15% when determining the value of an established larger company. Higher rates of return are used where the company being valued is viewed as having higher risk (e.g., a small company). In the next chapter, we will discuss how to estimate the cost of capital for your company.

Terminal Value

The terminal value represents what your company should be worth at the end of the forecast period (i.e., its enterprise value at that time). The terminal value is determined as follows:

Exhibit 3D : Terminal Value Calculation

	Annual Maintainable Discretionary Cash Flow Beyond the Forecast Period
Divided by:	Capitalization Rate
Equals:	Terminal Value

The terminal value is discounted (using the WACC discount rate discussed above) to its present value amount. When added to the present value of the discretionary cash flows during the forecast period, the result is the enterprise value of your company at a current date.

When estimating the annual maintainable discretionary cash flow beyond the forecast period, you should take into account expected longer term growth expectations, as well as the cyclicality of your company. A common error when applying the DCF methodology is to select a level of discretionary cash flow in the terminal value that is not maintainable over the longer term (e.g., it's at a high point of an industry cycle).

Annual maintainable discretionary cash flow should take into account the amount of sustaining capital expenditures that will be required in order to support and grow your company's revenue and cash flow over the long term. It's helpful to estimate the level of sustaining capital expenditure requirements by examining the estimated life of various assets by class (e.g., office equipment, vehicles, production equipment, etc.). This will help to ensure that the level of sustaining capital expenditures in the terminal value calculation is realistic. In addition, if further working capital will be required each year in order to support long-term growth, that should be factored into annual maintainable discretionary cash flow as well.

Capitalization Rates

The capitalization rate used in the terminal value calculation represents the inverse of a multiple of after-tax cash flow, as illustrated in Chapter 2. Recall for example from Exhibit 2G that a multiple of 10x after-tax cash flow was equivalent to an after-tax rate of return of 10%. The capitalization rate is calculated as follows:

Exhibit 3E : Capitalization Rate Calculation

	WACC Discount Rate
Deduct:	Long-Term Growth Rate
Equals:	Capitalization Rate

The long-term growth rate represents long-term inflationary growth and, in some cases, long-term real growth (i.e., growth in excess of inflation), where it can be justified. In this regard, it's important to recognize that the long-term growth rate refers to the ability for your company to generate returns in excess of its cost of capital, and by extension increase shareholder value. This is a key point. *While your company might be expected to grow its revenues and profitability, that does not necessarily mean the company is able to generate incremental shareholder value.* This point is illustrated in Chapter 6.

In a competitive marketplace, it's difficult to consistently achieve economic returns in excess of market rates of return over the long run. Hence, the long term growth factor adopted in the capitalization rate calculation normally falls in the range of 2% (which approximates long-term inflation expectations) up to about 5% (including both inflationary growth of about 2% and real growth of up to 3%).

By way of example, if you have used a nominal (i.e., including inflation) WACC discount rate of 13% and you believe that 3% long-term growth in your company is achievable (including both inflationary growth and real growth), you would use a capitalization rate of 10% (being 13% minus 3%).

An important point to note is the high degree of sensitivity that a relatively small change in the long-term growth rate can have on the determination of terminal value. Accordingly, you should carefully consider your long-term growth rate assumptions.

Example of the DCF Methodology

As an example of the DCF methodology, let's return to the case of Tasty Snacks Ltd. Assume that the company:

- currently generates revenues of $100 million. Tasty Snacks intends to undertake an expansion program that it expects will increase its revenues by 10% per year in each of the next 3 years. Revenues will grow thereafter at a long-term growth rate of 3% per annum;

- expects its EBIT (earnings before interest and taxes) margin to be around 7% of revenues. The EBIT margin is net of depreciation and amortization, with its forecast at 3% of revenues;

- will need to invest $9 million in new equipment next year in order to achieve its growth plan. Capital spending in the following years is estimated at $4 million per annum. Over the longer term, annual capital expenditure requirements will approximate depreciation;

- will require incremental working capital at a rate of 15% of revenue growth;

- has an income tax rate of 30%; and

- has interest-bearing debt of $15 million outstanding.

Assume that Tasty Snacks has computed its (after-tax) WACC discount rate to be 13%. Further assume that a long-term growth of 3% is achievable, and hence the capitalization rate used to determine the terminal value is 10%.

Under this scenario, the shareholder value of Tasty Snacks would be estimated at $35 million, as illustrated in Exhibit 3F:

Exhibit 3F : Valuation Estimate for Tasty Snacks—Discounted Cash Flow Methodology $(000), rounded

		Current Year	Forecast			
			Year 1	Year 2	Year 3	Thereafter
Revenues		100,000	110,000	121,000	133,000	137,000
% Growth			10%	10%	10%	3%
EBIT Margin	7%	7,150	7,700	8,470	9,310	9,590
Less: Income Taxes	30%	(2,150)	(2,310)	(2,540)	(2,790)	(2,880)
After-Tax Income		5,000	5,390	5,930	6,520	6,710
Add Back: Depreciation	3%	2,850	3,300	3,630	3,990	4,110
Deduct: Capital Spending		(2,850)	(9,000)	(4,000)	(4,000)	(4,110)
Deduct: Incremental Working Capital	15%		(1,500)	(1,650)	(1,800)	(600)
Discretionary Cash Flow		5,000	(1,810)	3,910	4,710	6,110
Capitalization Rate						10%
Terminal Value						61,100
Discounted Cash Flow						
# of Years Forward (Mid-Point)			0.5	1.5	2.5	2.5
Discount Factor at	13%		0.941	0.832	0.737	0.737
			(1,700)	3,260	3,470	45,000

Enterprise Value (rounded)	
Present Value of Forecast Period	5,000
Present Value of Terminal Value	45,000
	50,000
Deduct: Interest-Bearing Debt Outstanding	(15,000)
Equals: Shareholder Value	35,000

The discretionary cash flow for Tasty Snacks is *negative* $1,810,000 in Year 1 mainly due to capital spending requirements, and climbs to $4,710,000 by Year 3. Note how incremental working capital requirements significantly erode discretionary cash flow over the three-year forecast period.

The discretionary cash flow in Years 1 to 3 is discounted at the after-tax WACC discount rate of 13% per year, equating to a present value of approximately $5 million for the three years combined. (As a technical point, note that the discount factors are based on ½ years – i.e., Year 1 is 0.5 years forward, Year 2 is 1.5 years forward, and so on. This assumes that Tasty Snacks generates cash flows evenly throughout the year, as opposed to the end of the each year).

The annual maintainable discretionary cash flow beyond Year 3 climbs to $6,110,000, mainly because of reduced incremental working capital requirements, compared to the discretionary cash flow in Year 3. The discretionary cash flow beyond Year 3 is divided by the 10% capitalization rate (which assumes that discretionary cash flow will grow at a rate of 3% per year thereafter) to derive the terminal value of approximately $61 million. The terminal value amount is discounted at the 13% discount rate to derive a present value amount of $45 million. (As a technical point, note that the discount factor applied to the terminal value is based on 2.5 years forward. This is because the capitalization function in the terminal value calculation inherently assumes that the cash flows will be received one year later.)

The present value of the discretionary cash flows from Years 1 to 3 is added to the present value of the terminal value to derive the enterprise value of $50 million. Interest-bearing debt of $15 million is deducted to derive the shareholder value of $35 million.

Note how the enterprise value of $50 million is mainly represented by the terminal value component. This is not uncommon in the DCF methodology. This means that you must be cautious about your assumptions regarding the annual maintainable discretionary cash flow in the terminal value and the long-term growth rate.

Also note that the value conclusions derived for Tasty Snacks pursuant to the DCF methodology are the same as those derived pursuant to the valuation multiple approaches in Chapter 2. So why go through all the extra effort of preparing a DCF? First, the conclusions are not always the same, and the values derived pursuant to the DCF methodology normally are given greater weight due to the added rigor involved in the analysis. In addition, the DCF methodology incorporates all of the factors that influence value (including capital expenditures, working capital requirements and income taxes). By understanding how these variables impact value, you are in a better position to make decisions that positively impact shareholder value in your company.

Sensitivity Analysis

Valuation is a subjective exercise. It relies on forecasts that are subject to change, and an "educated guess" with respect to discount rates and capitalization rates. Therefore, you should incorporate a sensitivity analysis feature into your company's DCF model. This will provide you with a better understanding of the degree of variability in the valuation conclusions to changes in assumptions, and help you in assessing the risk profile of your company.

In the case of Tasty Snacks, a sensitivity analysis would reveal the following impact on both enterprise value and shareholder value:

Value Driver	Decline in Enterprise Value $millions
Discount Factor (Cost of Capital) Increases from 13% to 14%	5.1
Long-Term Growth Rate Decreases from 3% to 2%	3.1
EBIT Margin Decreases from 7% to 6%	9.2
Near-Term Revenue Growth Decreases from 10% to 9%	1.0
Incremental Working Capital Increases from 15% of Revenues to 16%	0.6
Income Tax Rate Increases from 30% to 31%	0.8
Long-Term Capital Spending Increases from 3% of Revenues to 4%	6.2

Based on this analysis, management of Tasty Snacks would be wise to concentrate their efforts on managing the company's cost of capital (i.e., risk profile), EBIT margin and capital spending, in order to ensure that shareholder value is not eroded.

Key Points to Remember

- Discretionary cash flow is net of operating expenses, capital expenditure requirements (growth and sustaining), income taxes and incremental working capital requirements, but before financing charges.

- The discount rate represents an *after-tax* weighted average cost of capital (WACC) based on the risk profile of your company and what is believed to be a normalized mix of debt and equity.

- The capitalization rate represents the WACC discount rate less a long-term growth rate.

- A meaningful valuation conclusion requires a realistic and internally consistent forecast.

- Incorporating sensitivity analysis into the DCF model will help you understand the impact on shareholder value against changes in assumptions, and therefore to better assess the risk profile of your company.

4 What is Your Cost of Capital?

Cost of capital represents the market's view of the required rate of return for an investment in your company, given prevailing economic and industry conditions, as well as your company's risk profile. A higher cost of capital is applied where higher levels of risk are perceived, or where you believe that the forecasted cash flows would be difficult to achieve.

Estimating your cost of capital is both subjective and complex. It is not my intention to overwhelm you with a bunch of formulas. However, you should understand the driving factors behind how the cost of capital for your company is determined. This is because *shareholder value is created where your company generates a return on its capital in excess of its cost of capital.* Therefore, by understanding how cost of capital is derived, you will be in a position to make more informed business decisions that help you build shareholder value within your company. Think about it this way: in order for your company to be profitable, you have to know the cost of producing the goods and services you are selling so that you know how much you have to charge to customers. Likewise, you need to have a good sense as to your company's cost of capital so that you can determine what return on that capital is needed in order to create shareholder value.

What Factors Determine Cost of Capital?

Recall that in Chapter 3 the concept of a discount rate was introduced, which is used in the discounted cash flow methodology. The discount rate is an after-tax weighted average cost of capital (WACC), which is based on what is believed to be a "normalized" mix of debt and equity. It follows that your company's cost of capital is comprised of two components:

1. the *unlevered return on equity*, which reflects the *operating risks* of your company. This takes into account prevailing economic conditions, the dynamics of the industry in which your company operates, and company-specific risks, such as the risk of losing key employees or major customers; and

2. a *normalized capital structure,* which represents the degree to which the market views that your company should be financed by debt vs. equity (i.e., the debt to equity ratio). A normalized capital structure may be quite different than the actual capital structure of your company.

Where debt can be used to finance your company, it serves to reduce its weighted average cost of capital, because debt financing is relatively inexpensive. Furthermore, interest expense is tax deductible, which makes debt financing even more appealing. However, the use of debt introduces the concept of *financial risk*, which is the risk that your company will not be able to meet its interest and principal repayment obligations.

Therefore, WACC represents a trade-off between the benefits of using lower cost debt and increased financial risk. As illustrated in Exhibit 4A, the use of some debt within your company will initially reduce its cost of capital. However, at some point, the risk of using debt outweighs the benefits, and your company's cost of capital begins to increase.

Exhibit 4A : Cost of Capital

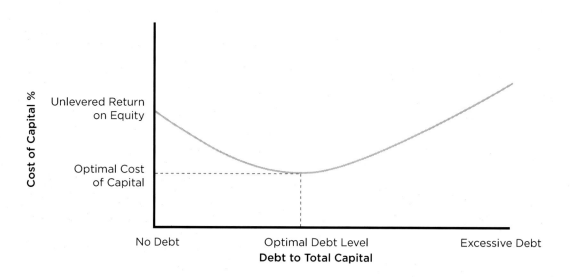

Estimating the Unlevered Return on Equity

The return on equity for public companies can be gauged by the trading price of the shares in the public markets. In most cases, investment bankers and stock analysts will use the *Capital Asset Pricing Model* (CAPM) and make adjustments for financial leverage to determine the unlevered return on equity. This is usually a technical exercise which can be found in most corporate finance texts. While CAPM is popular, it does have its drawbacks. The model lends itself well to large widely-held public companies, but the results can be distorted for small-cap public companies whose shares are thinly traded.

For privately-held companies (and small-cap public companies that don't rely on CAPM), the unlevered return on equity can be estimated by using a build-up approach as follows.

Exhibit 4B : Estimating the Unlevered Return of Equity

	Risk-Free Rate of Return
Add:	Public Equity Market Premium
Add:	Industry Risk Premium (If Any)
Add:	Company-Specific Risk Premium
Equals:	Unlevered Return on Equity

The starting point is the risk-free rate of return, which is usually represented by the yield to maturity on long-term government bonds. However, since we are dealing with equity rather than debt, we need to add a premium on account of the higher risk associated with equity investments in general. This is represented by the long-term premium returns that the stock markets have generated compared to the risk-free rate. In North America, that premium has historically been in the 4% to 6% range for the broad market index.

If your company operates in an industry characterized by higher than normal risk (e.g., due to extreme cyclicality or rapid technological change), it would be appropriate to increase the unlevered return on equity to account for industry-specific risks. In addition, you should consider company-specific risks, such as the degree of customer concentration, the strength and depth of your company's management team, the degree of competitive advantage in your company's product and service offerings and other factors. These factors are similar to those discussed in Chapter 2 – Factors Influencing Valuation Multiples.

However, unlike valuation multiples, the unlevered return on equity (and by extension the WACC discount rate) does not incorporate an adjustment for growth. This is because growth is incorporated in the discretionary cash flow against which the WACC discount rate is applied. Long-term growth is factored into the capitalization rate because the capitalization rate is applied against a point estimate of discretionary cash flow (i.e., annual maintainable cash flow beyond the forecast period).

Estimating your company's unlevered return on equity inherently is a subjective exercise, and a range is usually appropriate. It is important to be objective in your assessment, and not to dismiss your company's weaknesses and the risks that it faces. If you understate the risk inherent in your company you could end up with a meaningless, or misleading, value conclusion.

Companies with low levels of operating risk are usually characterized as established larger businesses that are not dependent upon a handful of customers or employees. It is not unusual for such companies to have an unlevered return on equity in the range of 12% to 15%. This represents an after-tax rate of return that should be applied to after-tax (i.e., discretionary) cash flows. Companies with high levels of operating risk are those that have economic dependence on a handful of customers, operate in a high-risk industry, or are dependent on the business owner or other individual employee. The unlevered return on equity for these types of companies commonly falls in the range of 16% to 25%, depending on the circumstances. Even higher rates of return are applied to early-stage and start-up companies, whose performance is not yet proven.

Continuing with our example of Tasty Snacks, let's assume that the current yield to maturity on long-term government bonds is 4% and that the public equity market risk premium is estimated at 5%. Given that Tasty Snacks is a food manufacturer, there is probably no premium on account of industry-specific risk. However, assume that the company is dependent on a handful of customers for the majority of its revenues, is smaller than its principal competitors, and is somewhat lacking in terms of the breadth and depth in its management ranks. These factors result in an estimated premium of 6% on account of company-specific risks. It follows that the unlevered return on equity for Tasty Snacks would be determined as follows:

Risk Free Rate	4%
Equity Risk Premium	5%
Industry-Specific Risk Premium	0%
Company-Specific Risk Premium	6%
Unlevered Return on Equity	15%

Estimating a Normalized Capital Structure

In theory there is an optimal capital structure for any given company. This represents the debt to equity ratio at which the cost of capital is minimized and therefore a company's enterprise value is maximized. However, in practice, it's hard to tell where that optimal point really is. We are not going to try to resolve that issue here. Rather, there are a few things to consider when estimating a normalized capital structure for your company.

In this chapter, we are addressing what a normalized level of debt would be for your company for the purpose of valuation. A normalized level of debt is driven by the perception of the market. You may decide to use more or less debt in your company than the estimated normalized amount, based on your business operating philosophy and personal preferences. These things are addressed in Chapter 10.

A normalized amount of debt does not mean the maximum amount of debt that your company could raise. Rather, it's based on a long-term view of your company's senior debt capacity, and should leave a cushion for unexpected events. Estimating a normalized amount of debt primarily is a function of two financial metrics, being:

1. the assets that can be offered as security; and

2. the cash flows available to satisfy interest and principal repayment obligations.

Most senior lenders look for security to cover their debt. While lending ratios can vary, it's not unusual to see the following ratios used by financial institutions:

- 75% of good accounts receivable (i.e., less than 90 days);

- up to 50% of inventory, depending on how saleable it is (e.g., raw materials, finished goods, etc.);

- 75% of real property; and

- up to 60% of the appraised value of machinery and equipment, depending on its nature.

Senior debt lenders will also look to lend a maximum amount based on your company's cash flow. Common ratios include: (i) debt to EBITDA; and (ii) times interest earned (EBIT divided by interest expense). Senior debt lenders will also require that your company meet certain covenants, such as a maximum level of debt to tangible net worth and a minimum level of working capital. These and other covenants can restrict the operations of your company. Lending amounts and financial covenant requirements fluctuate over time, based on economic and industry conditions and the general availability of credit.

Companies that have high debt capacity are those that have both stable cash flows and good security in the form of quality accounts receivable, saleable inventories and financeable fixed assets. These characteristics tend to be associated with established mid-size and large businesses, particularly those that operate in capital-intensive industries. Conversely, most high-risk and early stage companies do not have the ability to raise significant levels of debt, unless the debt is guaranteed by the business owner or another company.

Using our example of Tasty Snacks, assume that the company has the following balance sheet:

Exhibit 4C : Tasty Snacks Ltd.—Balance Sheet $(000)

Current Assets	
Accounts Receivable	16,000
Inventories	9,000
Prepaids and Other	2,000
	27,000
Intangible Assets	3,000
Fixed Assets	48,000
Accumulated Depreciation	(23,000)
	25,000
Total Assets	55,000
Current Liabilities	
Line of Credit	1,000
Accounts Payable & Accruals	12,000
Current Portion of Long Term Debt	2,000
	15,000
Long Term Debt	12,000
Total Liabilities	27,000
Equity	
Common Shares	1,000
Retained Earnings	27,000
	28,000
Total Liabilities & Equity	55,000

Further assume that senior lenders are willing to advance up to the following limits:

- not more than 2.5x EBITDA. Based on Tasty Snack's EBITDA of $10 million, this suggests senior debt lending of up to $25 million;

- a ratio of funded debt to tangible net worth of not greater than 1.5:1. Based on Tasty Snack's tangible net worth of $25 million, this suggests senior debt lending of up to $37.5 million (the determination of tangible net worth is discussed in the next chapter); and

- asset coverage of 75% of accounts receivable plus 50% of inventories, plus 50% of the appraised value of the company's machinery and equipment. Accounts receivable are $16 million, inventories are $9 million and let's assume that the appraised value of the equipment approximates its net book value of $25 million. It follows that the maximum lending under this test is $29 million.

Exhibit 4D : Tasty Snacks Ltd.—Debt Capacity Analysis $(000)

		Maximum Debt
Debt to EBITDA		
EBITDA	10,000	
Maximum Debt to EBITDA	2.5x	
		<u>25,000</u>
Debt to Tangible Net Worth		
Shareholder's Equity	28,000	
Less: Intangible Assets	(3,000)	
Tangible Net Worth	25,000	
Minimum Ratio	1.5x	
		<u>37,500</u>
Asset Coverage Test		
Accounts Receivable	16,000	
Coverage	<u>75%</u>	
	12,000	
Inventories	9,000	
Coverage	<u>50%</u>	
	4,500	
Fixed Assets (Appraised)	25,000	
Coverage	<u>50%</u>	
	12,500	
		<u>29,000</u>

Technically, Tasty Snack's maximum debt capacity would be the lowest of the three figures noted in Exhibit 4D, which is $25 million. However, it's generally prudent to have some cushion against unforeseen events, and to ensure that the company is not tripping its covenants for relatively minor shortfalls in operating performance. Taking all of these factors into account, management of Tasty Snacks estimates that a normalized amount of debt for the company is $20 million. Based on an enterprise value of $50 million, this represents a capital structure (i.e., debt to total capital ratio) of 40%.

Note that the normalized debt to total capital ratio is based on enterprise value as determined pursuant to a cash flow-based valuation methodology, and not the book value of a company's debt and equity. Therefore, the determination of a normalized debt to total capital ratio can become an iterative calculation, since increased debt capacity leads to a higher enterprise value. However, given that valuation is subjective, it's not worthwhile refining the number of iterations beyond two or three.

The Magic Formula for Cost of Capital

Rather than giving a long-winded explanation, we will jump to the "magic formula" for determining your company's cost of capital. Here it is:

$$WACC = K_U \times [1 - T \times D]$$

Where:

K_U is the unlevered cost of equity, which is a reflection of your company's operating risks;

T is your company's income tax rate, at which interest payments are tax-deductible; and

D is an estimate of the normalized debt to total capital ratio (i.e., debt to enterprise value) for your company.

Assuming a 30% tax rate, the WACC discount rate based on a range of unlevered rates of return on equity and normalized capital structure is as follows.

Exhibit 4E : WACC Discount Rates

	Unlevered Return on Equity						
Debt to Total Capital Ratio	12%	15%	20%	25%	30%	35%	40%
0%	12%	15%	20%	25%	30%	35%	40%
10%	12%	15%	19%	24%	29%	34%	39%
20%	11%	14%	19%	24%	28%	33%	
30%	11%	14%	18%	23%	27%		
40%	11%	13%	18%	22%			
50%	10%	13%	17%				
60%	10%	12%	16%				

Most companies with a high unlevered return on equity have little or no capacity to raise debt. While the WACC discount rate for any specific company can vary widely, depending on its risk profile and other factors, at the time of writing, it's not unusual to see WACC discount rates fall within the following ranges:

- 10% to 15% for larger established businesses with relatively low-risk profiles and the ability to use meaningful amounts of debt;

- 16% to 20% for established mid-sized companies with more modest risk profiles and some debt capacity;

- 21% to 25% for smaller, higher risk companies with limited debt capacity; and

• 26% to 40%+ for early stage and start-up companies with little or no debt capacity.

Exhibit 4F : General Weighted Average Cost of Capital Ranges

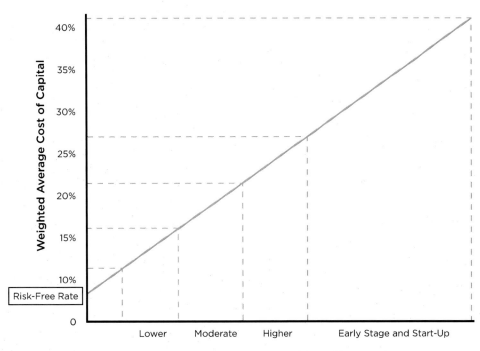

Returning to our example of Tasty Snacks, we saw that management estimated the unlevered cost of equity to be 15%, and a normalized capital structure comprised of 40% debt to total capital. Recall that Tasty Snacks has an income tax rate of 30%. It follows that the weighted average cost of capital for Tasty Snacks is calculated as follows:

$$\text{WACC} = K_U \times [1 - T \times D]$$

$$\text{WACC} = 15\% \times [1 - 30\% \times 40\%]$$

$$\text{WACC} = 15\% \times 0.88$$

$$\text{WACC} = 13\% \text{ (rounded)}$$

This is the discount rate applied against the forecast discretionary cash flows in the DCF model for Tasty Snacks in Chapter 3. Recall that the capitalization rate for Tasty Snacks is equal to the discount rate of 13% (above) less the assumed long-term growth rate of 3%, to arrive at 10%. The 10% capitalization rate was used in the terminal value component of the DCF methodology.

One of the nice things about the magic formula is that the WACC calculation is not overly sensitive to modest changes in capital structure assumptions. For example, if we had estimated a normalized capital structure for Tasty Snacks as being 35% rather than 40%, the resultant WACC for the company would have remained at 13% (rounded).

While the magic formula provides a precise answer for your company's cost of capital, it is only as good as the inputs. Since the tax rate is generally known, the subjective inputs are: (i) the unlevered return on equity; and (ii) the normalized capital structure. Furthermore, even if the WACC discount rate is properly determined, it's important that it be applied against a reasonable, internally consistent forecast of discretionary cash flows in order to develop a meaningful valuation result.

Again, any worthwhile valuation model should lend itself to sensitivity analysis so that you can understand the impact of a 1% change in the WACC discount rate on the value conclusions for your company.

Key Points to Remember

- Shareholder value is created where the return on capital exceeds the cost of capital.

- Your company's cost of capital is a function of its unlevered return on equity and a normalized capital structure.

- The unlevered return on equity reflects operating risks, taking into account economic conditions, industry dynamics and company-specific risks.

- The normalized capital structure is based on what the market believes to be a reasonable long-term debt to total capital ratio for your company.

- Senior debt lenders will look at your company's cash flow generation capabilities and the underlying assets that can be used as security when determining how much financing to advance (and hence a normalized capital structure).

5 What About the Balance Sheet?

Readers of financial statements usually are more interested in knowing their company's revenues and how much profit it made, as reflected on its income statement. The balance sheet often is not given adequate consideration. However, the balance sheet contains important information about the financial strength or weakness of your company and the amount of capital required in order to support its operations.

A misconception of some business owners and executives is that when they sell their company, they will receive the value of their company based on its cash flows (i.e., determined pursuant to a multiple of cash flow or discounted cash flow methodology), *plus* the retained earnings in their company. However, the convention in cash-flow based valuation methodologies is that the value conclusion includes a "normalized" balance sheet. This is because a certain level of working capital and fixed assets is required to generate the expected cash flows upon which the valuation is based.

In this chapter, we will discuss the role of the balance sheet in valuation. Chapter 9 will address how the balance sheet can be managed in order to build shareholder value within your company.

The Balance Sheet and Shareholder Value

As a general rule, a stronger balance sheet (as evidenced through the quantity and nature of your company's assets less its liabilities) supports a higher value being ascribed to your company. Financial strength is reflected in the discount rate or valuation multiple applied to your company's cash flows. This is because a stronger asset base means that your company can better access debt financing (where those assets can act as security). As illustrated in Chapter 4, the use of debt financing (rather than equity) helps to reduce your company's cost of capital.

Recall that shareholder value is determined by deducting outstanding interest-bearing debt from enterprise value. Shareholder value can be further segregated between tangible value (or *tangible net worth*, which is a measure of a company's physical assets less its liabilities) and intangible value (or *goodwill*). Specifically, intangible value is calculated as the difference between total shareholder value and tangible net worth.

Exhibit 5A : Calculation of Intangible Value

	Enterprise Value
Deduct:	Interest Bearing Debt Outstanding
Equals:	Shareholder Value
Deduct:	Tangible Net Worth
Equals:	Intangible Value

While a stronger balance sheet may increase your company's enterprise value, it does not mean that your company's intangible value is higher. This is because the higher enterprise value (and higher shareholder value) is offset by a higher level of tangible assets.

This brings us to a key factor in building shareholder value – managing invested capital. *It's not just how much cash flow your company generates, but rather how much cash flow it generates compared to what has been invested (i.e., the return on invested capital).* Think of it this way, would you rather own a company that generates $1 million cash flow per year on an investment of $5 million, or a company that generates $2 million per year on an investment of $40 million? The first company generates a return of 20%, whereas the second company only generates a return of 5%. While it seems obvious, it's astonishing how often business owners and executives focus only on their company's income statement and neglect the balance sheet, which reflects the capital required to generate the revenue and income results.

Tangible Net Worth vs. Intangible Value

Tangible Net Worth

Tangible net worth represents the equity invested in your company in the form of physical assets (e.g., working capital and fixed assets) less its liabilities. Tangible net worth is often referred to in banking and loan agreements, where certain borrowing covenants are based on minimum levels of tangible net worth for your company.

Tangible net worth excludes intangible assets that may be recorded on your company's balance sheet for financial accounting purposes. Examples of accounting intangibles include goodwill, customer lists, franchises and other non-physical assets. Accounting intangibles typically are recorded where your company acquired them from another party, rather than where they were developed internally. The value of these intangibles for accounting purposes might be wildly different from their economic value. Since we want to develop a true measure of economic worth, we start by setting aside any accounting intangibles. In some cases, a company might also have intangible liabilities for accounting purposes, such as deferred lease inducement costs, which are taken into income over time. These accounting liabilities do not represent a true economic liability, so likewise we start by setting them aside. It follows that the tangible net worth for your company is calculated as follows.

Exhibit 5B : Calculation of Tangible Net Worth

	Shareholders' Equity per the Balance Sheet
Deduct:	Intangible Assets on the Balance Sheet (At Their Net Book Value)
Add:	Intangible Liabilities on the Balance Sheet (At Their Net Book Value)
Equals:	Tangible Net Worth

Intangible Value

Intangible value represents the value of your company's assets that are in the form of brand names, licences, customer lists, proprietary knowledge and similar items. Intangible value is sometimes referred to as "goodwill". As noted above, the economic value of your company's intangibles may be materially different than their value for accounting purposes. In many cases, these intangible assets are not recorded on your company's balance sheet unless they were acquired in a transaction.

From an economic perspective, intangible value represents the difference between your company's shareholder value and its tangible net worth. Stated another way, the cash flows generated by your company first have to provide a return on its tangible net worth. Any excess cash flows are on account of intangible value.

Many business owners and executives believe that their company has intangible value because it has a good reputation, trained workforce, recognized brand names and other reasons. While all of these things may exist, it does not necessarily mean that their company has intangible value from an economic perspective. In other words, *just because your company has intangible assets does not mean that it has intangible value*. If the shareholder value of your company is less than its tangible net worth, then no intangible value exists from an economic perspective.

Which brings us to one of the central themes behind this book: *The creation of shareholder value ultimately rests in your ability to generate intangible value (or goodwill) within your company, as opposed to increasing its tangible net worth.*

Think about it this way. Let's say that you sell the shares of your company for $20 million. If the tangible net worth of your company is also $20 million, then all you have done is recovered your investment. It's like getting repaid an interest-free loan that you had to your company. While it's nice to get your money back, you haven't created shareholder value. However, if you received $20 million for the shares of your company and its tangible net worth is only $2 million, then you have received $18 million for intangible value. In other words, 90% of the sale proceeds are on account of goodwill.

Analyzing Your Balance Sheet

A useful exercise to determine the investment required to operate your company, and to properly calculate interest-bearing debt outstanding and tangible net worth, is to segregate your balance sheet into four components:

- Net operating assets;

- Intangible assets and liabilities;

- Redundant assets; and

- Financing.

Balance sheet segregation helps you in understanding the assets that are required to generate cash flows, how those assets are financed and where hidden value may exist (e.g., excessive working capital or redundant assets). *If you can reduce the amount of capital invested in your company without reducing cash flow or increasing risk, you can create shareholder value.*

Net Operating Assets

Net operating assets consist of your company's tangible operating assets (such as accounts receivable, inventories and fixed assets) less its operating liabilities (such as accounts payable and accrued liabilities). Net operating assets represent the assets required to generate discretionary cash flow for your company.

The value of your company, as determined pursuant to a cash flow based methodology, assumes that it has sufficient working capital and fixed assets to support its ongoing operations. Where actual working capital exceeds (falls short of) the required amounts, the difference is added to (deducted from) shareholder value otherwise determined. This is commonly the case in open-market transactions involving privately-held companies, where an adjustment to the purchase price is made if working capital delivered to the buyer at the closing date is different from levels that were agreed to. The determination of an appropriate amount of working capital for a given company inherently is subjective. Working capital and shareholder value is further discussed in Chapter 9.

Intangible Assets and Liabilities

In some cases, companies have recorded intangible assets on their balance sheet for accounting purposes, such as goodwill, franchise rights, customer lists and so on. These intangibles usually arise where a company acquired them from another party, rather them building them internally. As noted above, the accounting value of these intangible assets may be significantly different from their economic value. So our starting point is to segregate these accounting intangibles and disregard their value for financial accounting purposes. Their real economic value is reflected in the intangible value determined pursuant to a cash flow-based valuation methodology.

Similarly, any intangible liabilities (e.g., deferred leasehold inducements) should be categorized in the intangibles column, assuming that they do not represent a future cash outflow.

Redundant Assets

Some companies (more commonly privately-held companies), own assets that are not essential to their ongoing operations. These are referred to as *redundant assets*. Examples of redundant assets include vacant land and marketable securities. In order to qualify as a redundant asset, you must be able to remove them from your company without impacting the ability to generate revenue or cash flow. Further, redundant assets must be permanently redundant, and not the result of a temporary surplus (e.g., due to the seasonality of your company's operations).

Where redundant assets exist, their net realizable value should be added to the shareholder value of your company as otherwise determined. Furthermore, any costs or revenues associated with redundant assets should be removed from the cash flow stream being valued in order to avoid double-counting.

Financing

Financing includes both long-term and short-term interest-bearing debt obligations to banks and other lenders (e.g., operating lines of credit, term loans, mortgages and capital lease obligations). It also includes such things as loans and advances from shareholders and related parties, regardless of whether or not they are interest bearing.

If your company has cash on its balance sheet, that cash can be used to offset debt outstanding, so long as sufficient working capital remains in the business. If the application of cash against outstanding debt would result in negative or inadequate working capital, then some or all of that cash balance should be classified with net operating assets. If the amount of cash exceeds interest-bearing debt, the excess is added to shareholder value, assuming that it can be withdrawn from your company without negative implications.

Balance Sheet Segregation Example

As an example of a balance sheet segregation exercise, let's segregate the balance sheet for Tasty Snacks Ltd. (originally presented in Chapter 4) into its various components.

Exhibit 5C : Tasty Snacks Ltd.—Balance Sheet Segregation $(000)

	Total	Operating Assets	Intangibles	Redundant Assets	Financing
Current Assets					
Accounts Receivable	16,000	16,000			
Inventories	9,000	9,000			
Prepaids and Other	2,000	2,000			
	27,000	27,000			
Intangible Assets	3,000		3,000		
Fixed Assets	48,000				
Accumulated Depreciation	(23,000)				
	25,000	25,000			
Total Assets	55,000	52,000	3,000	0	0
Current Liabilities					
Line of Credit	1,000				1,000
Accounts Payable & Accruals	12,000	12,000			
Current Portion of Term Debt	2,000				2,000
	15,000	12,000	0	0	3,000
Long Term Debt	12,000				12,000
Total Liabilities	27,000	12,000	0	0	15,000
Equity					
Common Shares	1,000				
Retained Earnings	27,000				
	28,000	40,000	3,000	0	(15,000)
Total Liabilities & Equity	55,000	52,000	3,000	0	0

Note that most of Tasty Snack's assets are operating in nature. However, this analysis reveals that there is considerable net trade working capital ($15 million, being the difference between current operating assets of $27 million and current operating liabilities of $12 million). This may represent an opportunity to create shareholder value (which we will explore in Chapter 9). The total invested capital associated with the net operating assets is $40 million.

The intangible assets of $3 million are segregated, and the company has no redundant assets. Financing includes all forms of interest-bearing debt, which amounts to $15 million. The difference between total invested capital to support the net operating assets of $40 million, less $15 million of debt, represents the tangible net worth of $25 million.

The Hidden Value of Real Estate

If your company owns the real estate that houses its operations, that real estate should be viewed as a separate asset. The reason for this is that the multiples fetched by quality real estate (e.g., office buildings, warehouses, manufacturing facilities, etc.) often are greater than those applicable to operating companies, due to the difference in risk profile. This is particularly the case where the property can be readily leased or sold to a third party.

Consider the example of Tasty Snacks, which has normalized EBITDA of $10 million. Assume that the company owns the real estate that is used to house its operations, but that the property could be sold to a third party and leased back. Further assume that normalized rental cost for the property is $2 million per year. If the valuation multiple applicable to the business operations is 5x, and the multiple applicable to the real estate is 8x, then the enterprise value of the company would be $56 million, as illustrated in Exhibit 5D. This represents a $6 million premium over the $50 million enterprise value derived pursuant to the previous valuation estimates.

Exhibit 5D : Tasty Snacks Ltd.—Valuation Estimate With Segregation of Real Estate Assets $(000)

	Combined Basis	Segregated Basis	
		Operations	Real Estate
EBITDA	10,000	10,000	
Market Rent	n/a	(2,000)	2,000
Adjusted EBITDA	10,000	8,000	2,000
Multiple	5x	5x	8x
Enterprise Value	50,000	40,000	16,000
Combined Value		56,000	
Increase		6,000	

By viewing real estate as a separate asset, you will be better able to assess the true value of your company's operations, without that value being distorted due to real estate. It also helps to ensure that your company's real estate assets are managed appropriately to maximize their value as well.

Key Points to Remember

- Shareholder value is created through generating intangible value in your company, as opposed to increasing its tangible net worth.

- You can create shareholder value if you can reduce the amount of invested capital in your company (in the form of its tangible net worth) without impacting your company's cash flow or risk profile (i.e., its enterprise value remains unchanged).

- The economic value of your company's intangible assets may be significantly different from their accounting value.

- Segregate your balance sheet between operating assets, intangible assets and liabilities, redundant assets, and financing in order to better understand the capital investment requirements for your company.

- You should view real estate assets as a separate component of value within your company, given its different risk profile.

PART II VALUE CREATION

6 Principles of Value Creation

In Part I of this book, we discussed how value is measured and illustrated how the essence of creating shareholder value rests in the ability to generate intangible value within your company. Sounds simple? Well, you guessed it, there's more to consider. In order to generate intangible value, you need to develop a *competitive advantage* that affords your company the ability to earn a return on invested capital in excess of its cost of capital. Furthermore, that competitive advantage must be both *sustainable* and *transferable.*

In this chapter, we'll discuss the drivers of shareholder value and explore the concepts of creating a competitive advantage that is both sustainable and transferable. The following chapters in Part II will examine how a competitive advantage translates into a higher return on invested capital.

The *Shareholder Value Curve™*

We will begin by discussing what I call the *Shareholder Value Curve™*. The concept is relatively straight-forward. It begins with value measurement, which we explored in Part I. You need to understand how to properly measure shareholder value in order to assess whether or not progress is being made over time, and in order to identify the key drivers of shareholder value.

The next section of the *Shareholder Value Curve™* focuses on creating shareholder value. This requires that you undertake the initiatives that help to develop a competitive advantage within your company and leads to one, or a combination, of the following: (i) higher cash flow; (ii) lower risk; and/or (iii) reduced invested capital. This is the subject of Part II. As your company progresses along the curve, your focus should be on building *intangible value*.

The final section of the *Shareholder Value Curve™* deals with value realization. There are various avenues to value realization, which are covered in Part III. In order to realize the intangible value that is created within your company, you have to ensure that the competitive advantage you have developed is both sustainable and transferable to a new owner.

Exhibit 6A : The Shareholder Value Curve™

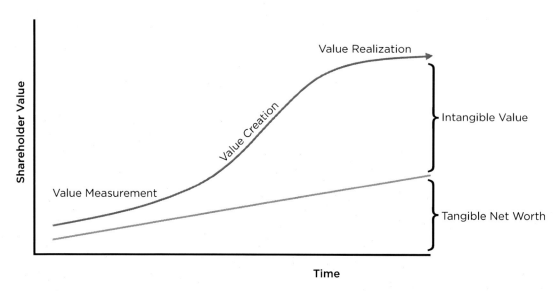

The Determinants of Shareholder Value

You will recall from Part I that your company's cash flow and risk profile (expressed as a discount rate or valuation multiple) are used to calculate its enterprise value. The amount of interest-bearing debt outstanding is deducted to determine shareholder value (which is comprised of tangible net worth and intangible value). It follows that there are three underlying components to shareholder value:

1. Your company's ability to generate *cash flow*, ultimately expressed as discretionary cash flow;

2. Your company's *risk profile*, which influences its cost of capital (or valuation multiple); and

3. The amount of *invested capital* in your company, which includes both debt financing and equity financing (in the form of tangible net worth).

Exhibit 6B : The Determinants of Shareholder Value

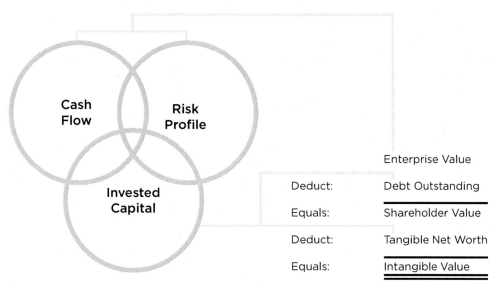

		Enterprise Value
Deduct:		Debt Outstanding
Equals:		Shareholder Value
Deduct:		Tangible Net Worth
Equals:		Intangible Value

The determinants of shareholder value are inter-related. Accordingly, the three elements must be assessed in combination, and not in isolation. The business decisions that you make will impact each of the three variables to a differing degree. *The key to creating shareholder value is to ensure that the benefits in the form of increased cash flow, lower risk or reduced capital requirements outweigh the drawbacks associated with generating those results.*

For example, implementing a growth strategy that increases cash flow, but which also serves to increase your company's risk profile and/or requires significant incremental capital, may result in an overall reduction in shareholder value.

This is why the discounted cash flow (DCF) methodology, illustrated in Chapter 3, can be an excellent tool for measuring and managing shareholder value. By considering the variables of the DCF methodology and how they interact, you will be in a better position to identify and undertake initiatives that enhance shareholder value within your company.

What Creates Intangible Value?

You will recall from Part I that the key to creating shareholder value is through building *intangible value*, as opposed to the accumulation of physical assets, which is reflected in your company's tangible net worth. From a technical perspective, intangible value is created where your company earns a return on its invested capital in excess of its cost of capital.

Consider the example of Tasty Snacks. In Chapter 3 we calculated the company's cost of capital (WACC) at 13%. We also assumed that long-term growth of 3% was achievable, for a capitalization rate of 10%. Tasty Snacks employs $40 million of total capital, comprised of $15 million debt and $25 million tangible net worth. Tasty Snacks should expect to generate $4 million of discretionary cash flow each year (growing at 3%) in order to provide an acceptable return on its total invested capital. If the company's annual cash flow exceeds $4 million, Tasty Snacks will generate intangible value, whereas if its cash flow falls below $4 million, shareholder value is eroded:

Exhibit 6C : Tasty Snacks Ltd. Cash Flow and Intangible Value $(000)

	Scenario 1	Scenario 2	Scenario 3
Discretionary Cash Flow	3,000	4,000	5,000
Cost of Capital	13%	13%	13%
Deduct: Long term growth rate	3%	3%	3%
Equals: Capitalization Rate	10%	10%	10%
Enterprise Value	30,000	40,000	50,000
Interest Bearing Debt Outstanding	(15,000)	(15,000)	(15,000)
Shareholder Value	15,000	25,000	35,000
Tangible Net Worth	25,000	25,000	25,000
Intangible Value	(10,000)	0	10,000

To reiterate the point from Chapter 5, *just because your company has intangible assets does not mean that it has intangible value*. Those intangible assets have to be grounded in a competitive advantage that allows your company to earn a return on invested capital in excess of its cost of capital, based on market rates of return. If shareholder value does not exceed tangible net worth, then it may be the case that your company has too much invested in tangible assets for the cash flow that it is producing, or that the operations of your company are not as efficient as they should be.

Where intangible value is positive, it's important to understand why that intangible value exists. There has to be an underlying reason why your company is worth more than its invested capital. In order to generate a return on capital that is in excess of market rates, your company must be doing something better than (or that distinguishes it from) your competitors. Otherwise, market forces will be such that any premium returns will be eroded.

Intangible value can be attributed to one or more benefits that your company enjoys which are not found on its balance sheet. For example:

- a well-recognized and trusted brand name;
- an established reputation for delivering high quality products and services;
- a skilled and trained workforce that would be difficult to replicate;
- a strategic location that reduces distribution costs;
- proprietary design efficiencies in production equipment; and
- a required government licence that creates a barrier to entry for competitors.

These things can provide your company with a competitive advantage that translates into shareholder value through one or a combination of the following:

- increased cash flow, which leads to higher profit margins;

- reduced risk, which reduces your company's cost of capital; or

- reduced capital requirements, which increases the return on invested capital for a given level of cash flow.

Consider the following examples:

Exhibit 6D : Examples of Shareholder Value and Competitive Advantage

Shareholder Value Driver	Competitive Advantage
Increased cash flow	• Your company can charge a premium for its goods or services because of its strong reputation or brand name recognition. Note that the premium price must offset the cost of maintaining that reputation or brand name. • Your company has developed proprietary production machinery or internal processes that give it a cost advantage over competitors (and resultant higher profit margins).
Reduced risk	• Your company has embedded itself with major customers in a way that creates a "barrier to exit" for those customers. • Your company has a strategic relationship with a key supplier of materials that are in short supply.
Reduced capital requirements	• Your company manages its working capital requirements more efficiently than its competitors. • Your company's strategic location allows it to minimize the capital expended on facilities and infrastructure.

The key is to develop a competitive advantage that results in your company earning a return on invested capital that exceeds its cost of capital, thereby generating intangible value.

Exhibit 6E : Competitive Advantage and Intangible Value

```
                    ┌──────────────────┐
                    │   Competitive    │
                    │    Advantage     │
                    └──────────────────┘
           ↙                  ↓                  ↘
  ┌───────────┐      ┌───────────┐      ┌───────────┐
  │   Cash    │      │   Risk    │      │ Invested  │
  │   Flow    │      │  Profile  │      │  Capital  │
  └───────────┘      └───────────┘      └───────────┘

  ┌──────────────────┐        ┌──────────────┐
  │   Return on      │   >    │   Cost of    │
  │ Invested Capital │        │   Capital    │
  └──────────────────┘        └──────────────┘

            ┌──────────────────┐
            │    Intangible    │
            │      Value       │
            └──────────────────┘
```

While it's nice to have a competitive advantage within your company, in order to realize on the intangible value created by that competitive advantage, it has to be both *sustainable* over the medium to longer term and *transferable* to a new owner. These concepts are explored in the next sections.

Creating a Competitive Advantage

Sustainability

In theory, over the long term, no company should be able to generate a return on invested capital in excess of market rates of return given that, over time, the supply and demand of goods and services within an industry should adjust to offset any temporary competitive advantage. Therefore, you have to assume that any competitive advantage that your company currently enjoys is not sustainable over the long term. While patents, licences or other forms of legal right may help to protect your market position in the near term, competitors can often work around these things and, ultimately, they do expire.

The key to creating a sustainable competitive advantage rests in your ability to implement the systems and culture that promote continuous *innovation* and *adaptation* within your company. This includes continuous product and service innovations, continuous improvements in manufacturing or delivery processes, and other initiatives that will allow your company to command premium prices for its goods and services and/or realize operating efficiencies better than your competitors. These things will help your company to earn a return on its invested capital in excess of its cost of capital, and therefore to generate and sustain intangible value.

For a brand name or reputation to sustain its value over the long term, it must be promoted and protected. If consumers have negative experiences with a product or service (e.g., due to quality issues) or if there is a highly publicized product recall due to safety concerns, that can be very damaging to the brand name or reputation.

Issues regarding sustainability often are associated with customers and employees. For a company to be successful over the long term and to create shareholder value, it needs to generate revenues. You can only go so far with cost-cutting measures. So the question becomes: How do you maintain and grow your customer base over time? As we will discuss in Chapter 8, a diverse base of repeat customers creates shareholder value. So ask yourself this: What are you doing in your company to create "barriers to exit", which will make it difficult for your customers to stop doing business with your company and deal with a competitor?

With respect to employees, while the use of employment contracts may help to reduce certain risks, such as misuse of confidential information or the blatant solicitation of customers, such contracts do not ensure that someone will remain in your company's employment. Long-term employment has much more to do with company culture, compensation structure, opportunities for advancement and a variety of other personal factors.

Transferability

In order to realize the shareholder value created within your company, it has to be transferable to a new owner. Otherwise, nobody will pay for it. So ask yourself whether a buyer would pay a premium for your company because they will benefit from the intangible value that you have created.

Where your competitive advantage stems from a legal right, such as a trademark, licence or patented technology, those assets are owned by the company and therefore transferable to a new owner (subject to expiry). However, other intangible assets may not be as easily transferable, such as customer relationships and employees. That's why it's important for your customers and employees to be loyal to the company itself, rather than a specific individual within your company, who may depart at some point.

A common mistake that many business owners make is to create too much dependence on their own involvement within their company. As a result, they become the key contact for major customers, the innovator of new products and so on. This is commonly referred to as *personal goodwill*. While the business owner may be able to use their personal skills and relationships to generate significant cash flow for their company, they are not creating shareholder value that can be readily transferred. This is because a buyer will not acquire their company without the continued involvement of the owner. Furthermore, in order to keep the owner involved and incentivized, a significant portion of the price paid for the company may come over time, or be contingent upon the achievement of future operating results. Consequently, the owner is stuck in their company, and becomes what I call a "stuckholder". They cannot even retire gracefully without devastating implications to their business.

Personal goodwill tends to develop over time as the business owner remains active in their company and deals directly with customers or is the person that comes up with most of the new innovations (such as in an engineering services firm). Many business owners find it difficult to let go because they believe that no one will serve their customers with the same degree of passion as they do, and because they are fearful of working themselves out of a job. This can be a disaster waiting to happen. Ideally, business owners should work to make themselves redundant to their company. While this scenario may not be personally appealing from an ego perspective, it does serve to maximize shareholder value and facilitate an exit.

As a test of whether personal goodwill resides within your company, try the following exercise. List your company's top 10 customers by sales volume. For each customer, ask yourself the following question: "If the owner got hit by a truck, which of these customers would still do business with my company?" If you find that several, or most, of your major customers would stop doing business with your company if the owner were no longer involved, you have a problem. Your company's value is too dependent on personal goodwill. The good news is that you now know you have a problem and can take steps to deal with it, such as grooming a strong management team and putting formal sales processes in place.

Personal goodwill can also arise in executives. For example, consider the case of a VP of Sales who has great relationships with their customers. This can be particularly problematic because your company may lose those customers if that executive leaves. What's more, where the executive does not have an incentive to build value within your company (i.e., they are not a shareholder or rewarded accordingly) their loyalty to your company may be minimal. While employment contracts, non-solicitation agreements and non-compete agreements (where enforceable) may help, they don't solve the problem. You need to ensure that the right systems, processes and people are in place to facilitate a transition of relationships.

Growth vs. Value

I want to end this chapter by discussing a common misconception among many business owners and executives – that growth leads to shareholder value. This is not necessarily the case. Consider the example of Tasty Snacks Ltd., which generates $10 million of EBITDA on $100 million of revenues. In Chapter 2 we estimated the enterprise value of Tasty Snacks at $50 million, based on a multiple of 5x EBITDA. Assume that management of Tasty Snacks decides to undertake an expansion initiative that will increase its revenues and EBITDA by 20%, to $120 million and $12 million, respectively. The cost of expansion (including capital assets and incremental working capital requirements) is $10 million. Assuming that a multiple of 5x EBITDA continues to be appropriate, Tasty Snacks has not created any incremental value, as illustrated below:

Exhibit 6F : Tasty Snacks Ltd. Growth vs. Value $(000)

	Before Expansion	After Expansion
EBITDA	10,000	12,000
Valuation Multiple	5.0x	5.0x
Enterprise Value	50,000	60,000
Cost of expansion		(10,000)
Net value		50,000
Value Created		0

This does not mean that management of Tasty Snacks has made a poor business decision by deciding to expand. Rather, it simply illustrates that the shareholders of the company are recovering their cost of capital and generating a market rate of return. That's not a bad thing. However, management of Tasty Snacks has failed to increase the intangible value of the company, and hence shareholder value, through its expansion initiative.

Growth initiatives are more likely to create shareholder value where one of three things occurs:

1. Operating efficiencies are achieved through growth initiatives, such as where fixed costs can be leveraged. In our example of Tasty Snacks, had EBITDA increased by 30% (to $13 million) instead of 20% ($12 million) because of better capacity utilization, then shareholder value would have been created.

Exhibit 6G : Tasty Snacks Ltd. Value Creation Through Operating Efficiencies $(000)

	Before Expansion	After Expansion
EBITDA	10,000	13,000
Valuation Multiple	5.0x	5.0x
Enterprise Value	50,000	65,000
Cost of expansion		(10,000)
Net value		55,000
Value Created		5,000

2. The risk profile of your company decreases, such as where the expansion initiative results in greater diversification. In our example of Tasty Snacks, if the valuation multiple increased to 5.5x EBITDA due to lower risk following the expansion, then shareholder value would have been created.

Exhibit 6H : Tasty Snacks Ltd. Value Creation Through Risk Reduction $(000)

	Before Expansion	After Expansion
EBITDA	10,000	12,000
Valuation Multiple	5.0x	5.5x
Enterprise Value	50,000	66,000
Cost of expansion		(10,000)
Net value		56,000
Value Created		6,000

3. The net operating assets of your company are managed so that incremental growth can be achieved without requiring significant incremental capital. In our example of Tasty Snacks, had the expansion initiative cost $5 million rather than $10 million, then shareholder value would have been created.

Exhibit 6I : Tasty Snacks Ltd. Value Creation Through Capital Management $(000)

	Before Expansion	After Expansion
EBITDA	10,000	12,000
Valuation Multiple	5.0x	5.0x
Enterprise Value	50,000	60,000
Cost of expansion		(5,000)
Net value		55,000
Value Created		5,000

Key Points to Remember

- The three drivers of shareholder value – cash flow, risk profile and invested capital, are inter-related. They must be managed on a collective basis.

- Generating intangible value requires that you develop a competitive advantage that will allow your company to earn a return on invested capital in excess of its cost of capital.

- Creating a sustainable competitive advantage requires that you develop an organization that is both innovative and adaptive.

- Beware of creating personal goodwill within your company that can impair the transferability of intangible value.

- Growth is more likely to translate into shareholder value where it results in operating efficiencies, risk reduction or reduced capital requirements.

7 Increasing Cash Flow

O ne of the most obvious ways to create shareholder value in your company is to increase the cash flow that it generates. However, as noted in Chapter 6, the creation of shareholder value requires that you consider (i) the amount of incremental capital required to generate incremental cash flow; and (ii) whether the initiatives undertaken to increase cash flow materially increase the risk profile of your company. A holistic view is important.

In this chapter we will primarily focus on operating cash flow (i.e., EBITDA), which is a function of revenues and operating costs. Cash flows relating to capital investment, working capital and financing are addressed in subsequent chapters.

Pricing Strategy

Revenue is a function of price and quantity. A higher price leads to a lower quantity sold, and vice versa. So you need to understand the relative change in quantity for a given change in price, or what is commonly referred to as the *price elasticity of demand* for your company's products and services. For example, if a 10% price decrease would result in a 20% increase in the number of units sold, then the price elasticity ratio is 2:1, and demand would be considered elastic. If you can raise prices without experiencing a significant drop in demand, then such a pricing strategy can often lead to significant incremental cash flow.

You may have considered reducing the price of the products and services that your company offers in an effort to increase revenues. However, it's important to go beyond the top line to determine whether price reductions will prove beneficial.

Here is an example: Tasty Snacks Ltd. sells its products for $10 per box, and each box costs $6 to manufacture and sell (i.e., variable costs). This leaves the company with a *contribution margin* (revenues less variable costs) of $4 per box. Tasty Snacks currently sells 10 million boxes per year, which translates into gross revenue of $100 million. After studying the market, management of Tasty Snacks concludes that reducing the price of its product by 10% (to $9 per box) will result in a 20% increase in volume (to 12 million boxes per year). While this strategy will lead to higher revenues, both profitability and cash flow will suffer, assuming that variable costs remain unchanged.

Exhibit 7A : Tasty Snacks Ltd. Impact of Pricing Strategy on Cash Flow $(000)

	Current Pricing	Proposed Pricing	Change
Price per box	$10.00	$9.00	-10%
Variable cost per box	$6.00	$6.00	0%
Contribution margin per box	$4.00	$3.00	-25%
Quantity sold (# of boxes)	10,000	12,000	20%
Total Revenue	100,000	108,000	8%
Total Variable Cost	60,000	72,000	20%
Contribution Margin	40,000	36,000	-10%

What went wrong? The problem is that, while Tasty Snacks cut the selling price of its product by only 10%, it decreased the contribution margin per box by 25% ($3 vs. $4). Assuming that the variable costs to manufacture and sell its products do not change, Tasty Snacks would have to sell 25% more boxes in order to break even. The break-even level would be even higher if the increased volume resulted in additional step costs (discussed below) in order to increase capacity.

The message here is simple. Maximizing revenues may not lead to higher cash flows or increased shareholder value. You need to understand the costs associated with revenue generation, which is discussed below. And remember, once you reduce the price for your goods or services, it's often difficult to implement a price increase later on.

Product and Service Offerings

One of the obvious ways to increase revenues and cash flow is to sell complimentary products and services. This can be an attractive business strategy because it can allow you to leverage existing customer relationships and help in building new ones. In many cases, the incremental costs incurred to sell complimentary products and services are minimal, which results in attractive incremental profit margins. Furthermore, your customers may find it more efficient to deal with a supplier that offers several products and services, rather than just a "one-trick pony". This can help to create customer "stickiness", which also reduces risk. Offering complimentary products and services can also reduce risk by providing greater diversification in revenues. We'll discuss this concept in the next chapter.

However, trying to offer too many complimentary products and services can backfire if it results in the sales process becoming too complicated or it creates inefficiencies in terms of production, distribution and selling.

Cost Management

As a starting point, it's important to distinguish between cost reduction and cost management. The focus of cost reduction is to increase short-term cash flow by eliminating certain expenses. While such measures may be necessary to avoid breaching bank covenants or staving off bankruptcy, they can often lead to an erosion of shareholder value over the long term. For example, cuts to marketing costs and R&D budgets may impair your company's competitive advantage over the long run, thereby decreasing its intangible value.

By contrast, cost management is an underlying business philosophy that charges business owners and executives to continually ask themselves whether the benefits relating to certain operating expenses outweigh the related costs, and whether it's possible to generate similar revenues through more innovative and adaptive means. Cost savings initiatives cannot be viewed in isolation from their impact on your company's risk profile or invested capital requirements.

Consider the following example. Tasty Snacks Ltd. is considering the elimination of two employees in its accounts receivable collections department, in an effort to save $100,000 per year, which translates into $70,000 per year after-tax (given its 30% tax rate). However, the company expects that this will cause accounts receivable to increase by 10%, from $16 million to $17.6 million, given the reduction in collection efforts. As illustrated in Exhibit 7B, the increased enterprise value of $0.7 million is more than offset by the higher capital requirements ($1.6 million), which results in an erosion of shareholder value.

Exhibit 7B : Tasty Snacks Ltd. Cost-Benefit of Employee Reduction $(OOO)

Annual cost savings	100	
Deduct: taxes at 30%	(30)	
After-tax savings	70	
Capitalization Rate	10%	
Increase in enterprise value		700
Existing Accounts Receivable	16,000	
Prospective accounts receivable (+10%)	17,600	
Increased capital requirements		1,600
Net gain (loss)		(900)

Cost Behaviour

Your company can earn a higher return on invested capital by managing operating costs and generating higher margins than its competitors. In order to make informed decisions with respect to cost management, you need to understand how the various costs in your company behave. You should ask yourself: "How do costs increase as revenue grows?" In this regard, costs can be segregated into three general categories:

1. Variable costs, which increase directly in proportion to sales volume. For example, the raw materials required to produce the products that your company sells;

2. Step costs, which increase as new capacity thresholds are reached. For example, if production capacity hits a certain level, it may be necessary to add a second shift and incur the cost of another supervisor; and

3. Fixed costs, which remain constant over the longer term. For example, the cost of securing a government permit.

Exhibit 7C : Cost Behaviour

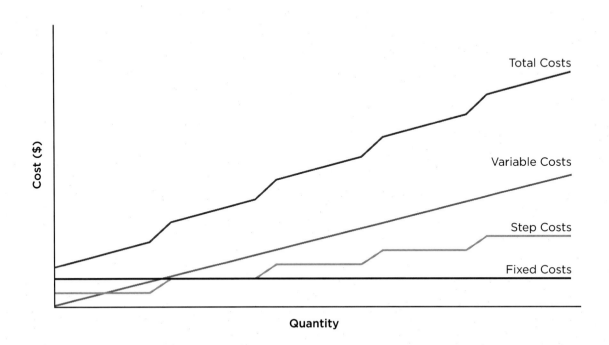

One of the best opportunities in cost management is to determine where you can realize operating leverage, so that revenues increase at a faster rate than costs, thereby expanding profit margins. A useful tool in this regard is to prepare profit and loss (P&L) statements by business segment, product or service line, customer account type, distribution channel, and so on, which will assist you in better understanding cost behaviour. In so doing, you should reclassify costs based on their behaviour, which is different than how your accountant classifies costs for the purpose of preparing your financial statements.

An example of a P&L for one of Tasty Snacks' product lines known as "Sweetums" is set out below. In this analysis, variable costs are directly related to the quantity produced. Steps costs are allocated based on the estimated relative capacity utilization within each expense category. Fixed costs are allocated based on a percentage of revenues.

Exhibit 7D : Tasty Snacks Ltd. Sweetums Product Line

	$(000)	%
Revenues	8,500	100%
Variable Costs		
Manufacturing	3,400	40%
Distribution	600	7%
Sales & Marketing	900	11%
Administration	0	0%
	4,900	58%
Contribution Margin	3,600	42%
Step Costs		
Manufacturing	700	8%
Distribution	800	9%
Sales & Marketing	400	5%
Administration	100	1%
	2,000	24%
Margin Before Fixed Costs	1,600	19%
Fixed Cost Allocation		
Manufacturing	300	4%
Distribution	100	1%
Sales & Marketing	200	2%
Administration	200	2%
	800	9%
Net Margin Before Taxes	800	9%

In the context of variable costs, leverage can be realized through economies of scale. For example, your company might be eligible for discounts from suppliers on raw materials by achieving certain purchasing thresholds. However, it's important to ensure that the higher volume required to receive purchasing discounts is not offset by higher step costs in order to accommodate that volume.

The polar opposite of variable costs is fixed costs. Intuitively, you should be able to leverage fixed costs within your company simply by generating more revenues. But it's not as easy as it sounds. Fixed costs only tend to remain fixed over a certain time horizon or sales volume. Even costs such as the President's salary, which may be fixed in the short term, tend to increase as a company grows. Over the long term, all costs become variable to some degree. It is just a matter of understanding how far you can go before those costs begin to rise.

The behaviour of step costs is probably the most difficult to understand, but it's an area where significant gains can be achieved. The key to understanding step costs lies in knowing where capacity constraints exist within your company. This can be done through such methods as time and motion studies. Capacity constraints can be observed in numerous areas throughout an organization, for example:

- production capacity of facilities and equipment;

- the available capacity on a company's fleet of delivery trucks;

- the number of customer accounts that a salesperson can handle; and

- the number of invoices that an accounting clerk can process.

For many companies, there is a tremendous opportunity to create shareholder value by generating incremental revenue without incurring incremental step costs, or by improving operating processes in order to remove a capacity constraint (e.g., more efficient billing systems). Such initiatives can generate operating leverage and therefore significant incremental cash flow.

However, you have to understand where all the relevant constraints within your company exist so that you don't inadvertently trigger incremental step costs in one part of your company for the sake of using up excess capacity in another area. For example, using up excess production capacity, but not having the distribution network required to accommodate the higher volume, may prove self-defeating.

Don't Forget About the Tax Man

Up to now, we've discussed increasing cash flow in terms of EBITDA. Capital spending and working capital are covered in Chapter 9. The other variable that forms part of discretionary cash flow is income taxes.

There are three parties to every transaction – the buyer, the seller and the government. To the extent that you can legally reduce or defer income taxes paid by your company, you can create shareholder value. Therefore, you should keep income taxes in mind when making business decisions.

Consider the following example. Tasty Snacks Ltd. believes that it's missing a sales opportunity because it under-stocks its inventory in certain regions. Management believes that the company could generate an additional $1 million every year in sales if the company increased inventory levels by $1.5 million. Tasty Snacks estimates that its incremental profit margin would be 20% on revenues. The company has an income tax rate of 30% and a capitalization rate of 10%.

On the surface, the proposed investment in additional inventory may seem attractive, because Tasty Snacks would generate incremental cash flow of $200,000 per year. However, on an after-tax basis, the company would erode shareholder value. This is because the incremental contribution margin is subject to tax, whereas the investment in higher inventories represents an after-tax amount.

Exhibit 7E : Tasty Snacks Ltd. After-Tax Impact of Investment $(OOO)

Incremental revenue per year	1,000,000
Incremental profit margin at 20%	200,000
Income taxes at 30%	(60,000)
Annual after-tax benefit	140,000
Capitalization rate	10%
Increase in enterprise value	1,400,000
Increased inventory investment	(1,500,000)
Net benefit (loss)	(100,000)

Tax efficiency also comes into play when looking at corporate acquisitions or the sale of your company. We'll discuss these issues in subsequent chapters.

Key Points to Remember

- Focus on the contribution margin, not gross revenues, when making pricing decisions.

- Offering complimentary products and services can help in leveraging existing customer relationships and provide additional diversification.

- Focus on cost management rather than purely cost reduction, which could lead to making decisions that impair intangible value within your company.

- Understand how various costs behave within your company and try to increase cash flow by utilizing excess capacity where possible.

- Don't forget about the impact of taxation when making business decisions.

8 Risk Management

Shareholder value can be created by reducing the risk profile of your company, so long as (i) cash flow is not compromised; and (ii) the invested capital required to do so does not offset the benefits of risk reduction.

A lower risk profile will reduce your company's cost of capital (i.e., its discount rate) or, alternatively, increase its valuation multiple. Either way, the enterprise value of your company will increase, which in turn will lead to higher shareholder value.

When risk management is discussed in this chapter, we are referring to operating risk, as opposed to financial risk. Recall that the two concepts are independent. Operating risk is a reflection of prevailing economic conditions, the industry in which your company operates and company-specific risks, such as losing key employees or major customers. Financial risk, on the other hand, relates to how your company is financed – which is discussed in Chapter 10.

Identifying Operating Risks

The first step in managing risk is to identify the various risks faced by your company. Operating risks can be categorized as being either *internal* (i.e., residing within your company, or "weaknesses") or *external* (i.e., residing outside of your company, or "threats"). You can also think about risk in terms of whether it relates to your company's *inputs* (i.e., materials, machinery, people and capital), *processes* (i.e., the conversion of inputs to products and services, and the operations of your company), or *outputs* (i.e., threats to your company's customer base or product and service offerings). The various risks that might be faced by your company could be categorized in an operating risk grid as follows:

Exhibit 8A : Operating Risk Grid

	Internal (Weaknesses)	External (Threats)
Input	• Limited number of trained employees • Capacity limitations	• Reliance on a single supplier for a critical raw material • Availability of capital to support your company's growth plans
Process	• Inadequate data recovery systems • Potential liability due to inadequate corporate governance	• Rapidly changing manufacturing technology • Changes to industry regulations that will lead to higher costs
Output	• Reliance on a handful of products or services to produce the majority of revenues • Patented product design is near expiration	• Competitive developments • Substitute products or services • Customer concentration • Changing economic conditions • Foreign exchange risk

An objective and comprehensive process of risk identification is critical in order to understand where your company is exposed to potential downfalls. Starting with the right information is fundamental to making informed business decisions. So good risk management begins with good information management.

Business owners and executives frequently understate the risks to which their company is exposed. It's human nature to be optimistic and, consequently, to dismiss potential threats when looking from the inside out. When identifying and assessing various operating risks, it's often helpful to engage outside assistance from an organization that understands the industry in which your company operates and can provide objective and meaningful insight. But no matter how hard you try, there is always the concept of "risk risk". That is, the risk of not knowing what risks your company is exposed to.

Risk Assessment

Once you have identified the operating risks facing your company, you need to assess their potential impact in terms of the likelihood that they will occur and the severity of the outcome. This can be done with the help of a *risk assessment matrix*.

Exhibit 8B : Risk Assessment Matrix

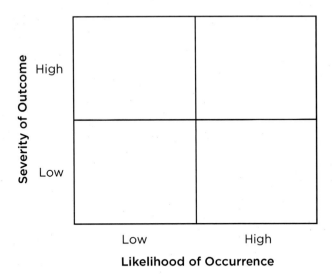

Risk assessment should be thought of in terms of the potential reduction in shareholder value. For example:

• reduced cash flow due to lost revenue or additional operating costs;

• a higher cost of capital due to a higher risk profile resulting from greater concentration of customers or potential variability of operating results; and

• higher capital investment requirements to compensate for changing market conditions or operating inefficiencies.

The impact of these things can be quantified with the assistance of the sensitivity analysis feature in your discounted cash flow valuation model.

Risk assessment is important because it allows you to assess the cost benefit associated with risk mitigation strategies (discussed below). Risks that are assessed as having a high likelihood of occurrence and high severity of outcome should be given priority. On the other hand, you might decide to live with risks that are categorized as having a low likelihood of occurrence and low severity of outcome.

Remember that risk identification and risk assessment are not static. These things change over time, so they have to be revisited on a regular basis in order to ensure that your company's risk management initiatives are being kept current.

Risk Mitigation Strategies

Your objective should not be to eliminate all of the risks facing your company. Attempting to do so would be cost-prohibitive, and likely impair the entrepreneurial spirit that's required for your company to maintain its competitive advantage. Rather, it's a matter of making an informed decision regarding the trade-off between:

- the potential reduction to your company's risk profile, in terms of a lower cost of capital (or higher valuation multiple); and

- the cost of implementing the risk reduction measures, in terms of the reduction in cash flow or increased capital required.

Returning to our example of Tasty Snacks Ltd. in Chapter 4, one of the major risks facing the company was inadequate breadth and depth in its management team. The owner of Tasty Snacks is considering hiring two senior management individuals in order to mitigate this risk, at a combined cost of $500,000 per year. Improved management succession is expected to reduce the company's cost of capital (WACC) by one percentage point, from 13% to 12%. By extension, the capitalization rate declines from 10% to 9%. The potential impact on the enterprise value of the company is as follows:

Exhibit 8C : Tasty Snacks Ltd. Impact of Management Succession Initiative $(000)

	Existing Risk Profile	Prospective Risk Profile
Current EBITDA	10,000	10,000
Cost of new management		(500)
Prospective EBITDA	10,000	9,500
Depreciation/capex	(2,850)	(2,850)
Pretax cash flow	7,150	6,650
Income taxes	(2,150)	(2,000)
Discretionary cash flow	5,000	4,650
Capitalization rate	10%	9%
Enterprise value	50,000	51,700
Interest bearing debt outstanding	15,000	15,000
Shareholder value	65,000	66,700
Net Benefit		1,700

Note that the analysis is conducted on an after-tax basis in order to capture all of the elements of shareholder value. In this example, the reduction in cash flow (net of the associated tax savings) is more than offset by the benefit of a lower risk profile. Therefore, from an economic perspective, the management succession initiative would increase shareholder value.

Risk mitigation is important from a revenue standpoint as well. Not every dollar of revenue makes the same contribution to shareholder value. Apart from the cost associated with generating revenues, it's also important to consider the risk attaching to your company's revenue stream. Increasing the stability and predictability in revenues (e.g., through maintenance contracts, supply agreements, etc.), will reduce your company's risk profile and increase its shareholder value.

Internal vs. External Risks

Companies can take measures to control their internal risks, but must adapt to external risks. External risks are common to companies operating within an industry (e.g., government regulations, technological change and so on). Therefore, *your company can create and maintain a competitive advantage by being innovative and adapting to external changes in an efficient and effective manner.*

Becoming an adaptive company means keeping your eye on the market in terms of trends and developments so that you know where things are headed. It's like hockey great Wayne Gretzky said, "Don't go to where the puck is now, go to where it's going to be."

Remember that over the long term, building shareholder value is akin to building intangible value, which rests in your ability to develop a competitive advantage that is both sustainable and transferable. Creating an innovative and adaptive company is fundamental to this initiative. Your focus should be on continuous improvement in every aspect of your company's operations, from product and service offerings to customer relations, to operating procedures, etc.

This is easier said than done. Innovation and adaptability have much more to do with corporate culture than with systems and processes. It can be challenging if employees believe that innovation and adaptation could result in their becoming redundant to the company and consequently unemployed. However, you need to help your employees to understand that if they continually resist innovation and adaptation, the entire company will lose its competitive advantage, and their jobs are more likely to be at risk as a result. Alternatively, where innovation and adaptation lead to increased shareholder value, the positive impact of that development tends to snowball, thereby reinforcing the benefits of such a culture.

Exhibit 8D : Company Culture and Shareholder Value

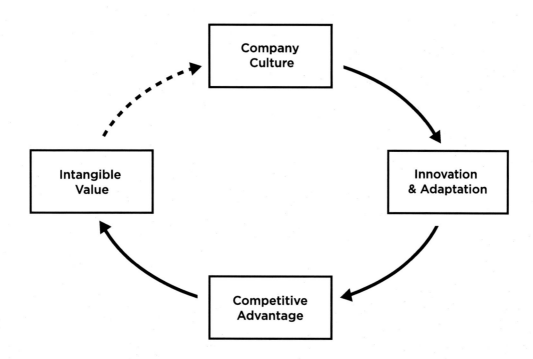

So ask yourself three key questions:

1. Where is the competitive advantage in my company today?

2. How do I maintain and improve the sustainability and transferability of that competitive advantage?

3. What developments could occur that would erode that competitive advantage?

Remember that your competitive advantage (be it proprietary products, efficient processes, technical know-how, etc.) must lead to higher cash flows (higher revenues or lower costs), lower risk (e.g., barriers to exit for customers) or more efficient capital utilization (working capital and fixed assets) than your competitors in order to earn a return on capital in excess of your cost of capital, thereby generating intangible value.

The Benefits of Diversification

A lot of risk is created where a company has too much concentration in terms of its customer base, product and service offerings, management team and other key operating parameters. Companies that are adequately diversified have a lower cost of capital compared to those that are not.

When assessing the level of concentration and diversification within your company, you should consider the following parameters:

- **Customer base.** In an ideal world, no individual customer should represent more than 10% of your company's revenues. It's also helpful to know what percentage of your customers comprise 50% of your company's revenues;

- **Product and service offerings.** Ideally, you should not be relying on a handful of specific product or service offerings to generate the majority of your revenues. Furthermore, a meaningful portion of your company's revenues should be generated through product and service offerings that have been introduced within the past few years. This illustrates innovation and adaptability;

- **Management team.** You should have identified one or more possible successors for each key management position within your company. Furthermore, you should assess the degree to which key customer accounts and technical knowledge are diversified among your employee base;

- **Geographic.** This is measured by the degree to which your company's revenues are generated within a particular country or region. Geographic concentration can leave your company exposed to local economic and political conditions; and

- **Suppliers.** This is measured by the degree to which raw materials and other key inputs are sourced through one or a few suppliers. Supplier concentration is less of an issue where alternate sources of supply are readily available.

While diversification helps to reduce risk, there is a trade-off. Increased diversification can result in added complexities within your organization (e.g., managing multiple divisions) and operating inefficiencies (e.g., production changeovers, loss of economies of scale, and so on).

You may recall that during the 1980s it was popular for large public companies to be conglomerates, based on the assumption that the public equity markets would reward them with a lower cost of capital due to diversification. However, by the late 1990s, most of these conglomerates had spun off major parts of their operations as public equity investors began to favour "pure play" firms that specialized in one industry segment, and instead obtained diversification by selecting different companies in their stock portfolio.

Diversification tends to work on the basis of diminishing returns. The initial benefits can be significant in terms of risk reduction. Your company might also benefit from offering complimentary products and services that help in utilizing excess capacity (and therefore increasing cash flow). However, at some point, the incremental costs related to added organizational complexities and inefficiencies outweigh the incremental gains. *The key to building shareholder value is to strike the right balance between using diversification to reduce your cost of capital vs. the incremental cash flow and invested capital required to achieve that diversification.*

Exhibit 8E : Diminishing Returns from Diversification

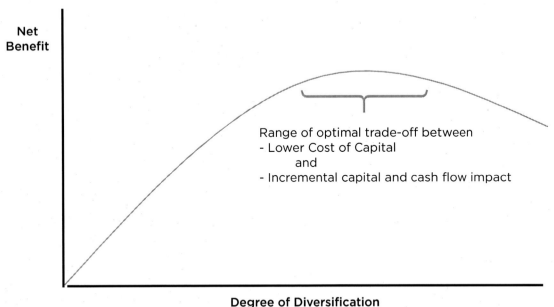

Net Benefit

Range of optimal trade-off between
- Lower Cost of Capital
  and
- Incremental capital and cash flow impact

Degree of Diversification

Key Points to Remember

- Identify the risks faced by your company by considering both internal and external risks, and whether they relate to your company's inputs, processes or outputs.

- Conduct an objective assessment as to the likelihood that the risks will occur and the severity of the impact that they could have on shareholder value.

- When considering risk mitigation strategies, consider the trade-off between a lower risk profile (i.e., lower cost of capital) and the incremental costs in terms of both cash flow (net of tax) and capital requirements.

- Ultimately, risk mitigation requires that you instill a culture needed to create an innovative and adaptive organization that makes your company's competitive advantage both sustainable and transferable.

- Diversification is a key element of risk management, but the benefits of diversification must be weighed against the costs associated with added complexity and inefficiencies.

9 Asset Management

In Chapter 5, we discussed how your company's intangible value is calculated as the difference between its total shareholder value (determined pursuant to a multiple of cash flow or discounted cash flow methodology) and its tangible net worth. It has also been stated repeatedly that the key to creating shareholder value is to generate intangible value within your company. It follows that intangible value can be increased either by increasing shareholder value for a given level of tangible net worth, or reducing tangible net worth for a given level of shareholder value.

This chapter deals with managing the net operating assets (i.e., net working capital and fixed assets) used in your company as a means of reducing tangible net worth without impairing its enterprise value (or shareholder value), thereby generating intangible value.

Working Capital Management

Net working capital is calculated as the difference between current assets and current liabilities. In the context of this chapter, we will focus on *net trade working capital*, which sets aside any financing component included in short-term liabilities (such as bank operating loans) and excess cash, as well as any non-operating current assets (i.e., redundant assets). The major components of net trade working capital typically include accounts receivable, inventories, prepaid expenses, accounts payable and accrued liabilities. Recall from the balance sheet segregation exercise in Chapter 5 that net trade working capital is classified as a component of the net operating assets used in your company. The working capital portion of the segregated balance sheet for Tasty Snacks is reproduced below.

Exhibit 9A : Tasty Snacks Ltd. Working Capital Segregation $(000)

	Total	Operating Assets	Intangibles	Redundant Assets	Financing
Current Assets					
Accounts receivable	16,000	16,000			
Inventories	9,000	9,000			
Prepaids and other	2,000	2,000			
	27,000	27,000			
Current Liabilities					
Line of credit	1,000				1,000
Accounts payable & accruals	12,000	12,000			
Current portion of term debt	2,000				2,000
	15,000	12,000	0	0	3,000
Net	12,000	15,000	0	0	(3,000)

Working capital management is one of the most overlooked ways for increasing shareholder value. In fact, mismanagement of working capital can quickly result in a company's demise – particularly for rapidly growing companies that are focused on revenue generation and do not pay heed to the cost associated with increasing accounts receivable and inventories. Even where current assets can be financed by a bank operating line, you should not overlook the cost of that financing, and the overall cost of capital for an investment in your company. Remember that working capital represents after-tax dollars that are tied up in your company.

Let's revisit the example of Tasty Snacks. The company's net trade working capital is currently $15 million, which represents 15% of revenues of $100 million. If management were able to implement initiatives to reduce its working capital levels to 12% of revenues, then Tasty Snacks could generate $3 million in cash. That cash could be applied against outstanding debt, which would result in a direct increase in shareholder value. In addition, as the company grows, it would require less incremental working capital to support that growth. This would translate into a $1.7 million increase in the enterprise value of Tasty Snacks, which would flow through to higher shareholder value. Consequently, effective working capital management would cause Tasty Snack's shareholder value to increase from $35 million to $39.7 million.

Exhibit 9B : Tasty Snacks Ltd. Impact of Working Capital Management on Shareholder Value $(000)

	Current Year	Forecast Year 1	Year 2	Year 3	Terminal Value
Revenues	100,000	110,000	121,000	133,000	137,000
Working Capital at 15% of revenues	(15,000)	(1,500)	(1,650)	(1,800)	(600)
Working Capital at 12% of revenues	(12,000)	(1,200)	(1,320)	(1,440)	(480)
Difference	3,000	300	330	360	120
Capitalization Rate					10%
Capitalized value					1,200
# of years forward (mid-point)		0.5	1.5	2.5	2.5
Discount factor at 13%		0.941	0.832	0.737	0.737
		282	275	265	884
Existing working capital converted to cash	3,000				
Incremental enterprise value (rounded)	1,700				
Total increase in shareholder value	4,700				
Existing shareholder value (Exhibit 3F)	35,000				
Pro-forma shareholder value	39,700				

This analysis assumes that reduced working capital levels would not impair the ability of Tasty Snacks to reach its revenue and cash flow forecasts, or adversely affect the risk profile of the company. Again, all factors have to be considered when assessing shareholder value.

Working Capital Ratios

There are a myriad of ratios that can be used to help assess the working capital levels of your company. Some of the more common include the following:

Exhibit 9C : Working Capital Ratios

Current ratio: = $\dfrac{\text{Total current assets}}{\text{Total current liabilities}}$	Provides a high level view of your company's liquidity and solvency. If the current ratio dips below 1:1, your company technically is unable to meet its current obligations as they come due
Quick ratio = $\dfrac{\text{Cash + accounts receivable}}{\text{Total current liabilities}}$	Also measures near-term liquidity. This ratio focuses on cash and near-cash assets that are readily available to satisfy current obligations. Other current assets, such as inventories and prepaid expenses, often take time to convert into cash
Net trade working capital as a percentage of revenues	Helps you in assessing how much additional net trade working capital (e.g., accounts receivable and inventories, net of accounts payable) your company will require in order to support revenue growth

The calculation of these and other working capital ratios (discussed below) can help in detecting trends and anomalies that may suggest underlying issues exist. These ratios can also be compared to other companies within your industry, to assess whether your company is managing its capital more efficiently than industry norms.

However, ratio analysis has to be used with caution. You need to consider whether the results are impacted by seasonality. In addition, when comparing your company's ratios to those of other companies, you need to consider whether differences in product and service offerings, geographic coverage and accounting policies will distort the results.

Specific Working Capital Accounts

Cash Management

Recall from the balance sheet segregation exercise in Chapter 5 that cash is usually classified as an offset to debt financing. This inherently assumes that cash can be applied to reduce the amount of debt outstanding, and that doing so would not result in a net trade working capital deficiency. Where cash on hand exceeds outstanding debt, the excess is usually treated as a redundant asset and added to shareholder value, assuming that it can be readily withdrawn from your company. However, where the remaining net trade working capital (after offsetting or removing excess cash) would be inadequate to support the operations of your company, some or all of the cash on hand should be viewed as a net operating asset. As a practical matter, most companies need some cash (or a line of credit) in order to operate. Therefore you need to assess the ongoing cash requirements in your company.

A useful measure for assessing the effectiveness of cash management is the *cash cycle* of your company. Cash cycle refers to the number of days that it takes to convert your company's goods and services into cash. It is calculated as follows:

Exhibit 9D : Calculation of Cash Cycle

	Days in Inventory
Add:	Days in Accounts Receivable
Deduct:	Days in Accounts Payable
Equals:	Cash Cycle (days)

The value of your company is based on the cash flow that it generates. Therefore, cash management is central to value creation. Some business owners and executives like to keep excess cash on hand as a cushion against uncertainty. As noted above, from a valuation standpoint, cash on hand in excess of what is needed to operate your company is added to shareholder value as a redundant asset. Just be careful that maintaining surplus cash does not result in becoming lax on cash management within your company. A good practice for private companies is for the shareholders to withdraw excess cash on hand and then loan it back to the company, so long as this can be done on a tax-deferred basis. This can help in creditor protection and create an awareness within the company that invested capital requires an adequate return.

In the context of a public company, the public equity markets sometimes overlook cash as a component of value, and rather simply focus on multiples such as price to earnings. Where there is no use for the excess cash in the foreseeable future, it may be wise to consider a share buyback or a special dividend. However, caution is warranted because once the cash is gone from a public company, it can be hard to replace.

Accounts Receivable

Many companies have a considerable amount of money tied up in accounts receivable.

Your company should have clear credit and collection policies and ensure that they are communicated to customers and enforced. It may even be worthwhile hiring an individual just to ensure that accounts receivable are collected on a timely basis. In the example in Exhibit 7B, Tasty Snacks was looking to save $100,000 per year by eliminating two collection clerks. That initiative would result in a $1.6 million increase in accounts receivable due to reduced collection efforts, thereby causing a net reduction in shareholder value.

Reducing the level of accounts receivable can also help in maintaining the quality of these accounts (i.e., reducing outstanding accounts over 90 days), which helps in maintaining a line of credit that is secured by accounts receivable.

Some companies offer discounts for prompt payment, such as 2% for payment in 10 days, net 30 days. While this tactic may appear attractive, it can be very costly. This particular incentive implies that a customer is given a discount of 2% for paying 20 days early, which translates into an annualized cost of about 36%. Furthermore, once prompt payment discounts have been offered, they are difficult to retract without negative repercussions from customers, even those that didn't take advantage of the discount!

In order to collect promptly, it's important to invoice promptly. You should ensure that your company's practice is such that there is minimal delay in billing customers. If you can invoice in advance for your company's products and services, that approach is ideal. While advance billing leads to deferred revenues, this practice goes a long way to reducing net trade working capital and increasing shareholder value.

Some useful metrics to keep in mind when managing accounts receivable are as follows:

Exhibit 9E : Accounts Receivable Ratios

Days sales outstanding $= \dfrac{\text{average accounts receivable}}{\text{revenues}} \times 365$	Measures the number of days that it takes to collect outstanding accounts from your customers. It should be compared against your stated collection policy
Accounts aging analysis	Tracks the percentage of accounts receivable that are current, 30 days overdue, 60 days overdue and more than 90 days overdue. This analysis can be a leading indicator of pending collection problems
Accounts receivable concentration	Examines the percentage of total receivables represented by specific customer accounts. If the percentage of accounts receivable for a major customer is materially greater than the percentage of total revenue for that customer, it may signal possible collection problems
Bad debt expense as a percentage of revenues	Trends in this ratio can signal credit or collection issues

Inventory

Inventory management is an important initiative for companies that sell products. It's easy for inventories to grow to excessive levels. But there can be a trade-off here, because inadequate inventories may lead to lost sales opportunities. Therefore, inventory control practices should set a balance between carrying cost and opportunity cost.

Some useful measures of inventory management are as follows:

Exhibit 9F : Inventory Ratios

Days in inventory $= \dfrac{\text{average inventory}}{\text{cost of sales}} \times 365$	Measures the number of days that it takes to turn inventory into revenue
Inventory aging analysis	Examines the percentage of inventory that has been on hand under 30 days, 30 to 60 days and over 60 days. Trends in this analysis serve as an indicator of aging inventory
Inventory composition	Examines the proportion of inventory represented by raw materials, work in progress and finished goods
Inventory write-offs as a percentage of revenues	A growing trend may indicate inventory management problems
Lost sales due to inadequate inventory available	This analysis can indicate that inventory controls are too stringent, or that the wrong mix of inventories is being kept in stock
Order time	Represents the average length of time between when orders are received from customers and when the goods are shipped. A growing trend in order time can be an early indicator of customer dissatisfaction and potentially lost orders

Accounts Payable and Accrued Liabilities

You can reduce your company's net trade working capital requirements by stretching accounts payable, so long as it does not result in negative repercussions with suppliers. An exception to this rule is where suppliers offer discounts for prompt payment. As illustrated above, prompt payment discounts of 1% or 2% can result in significant savings where those rates are annualized.

Some useful metrics in managing accounts payable are as follows:

Exhibit 9G : Accounts Payable Ratios

Days in Accounts Payable $= \dfrac{\text{average accounts payable}}{\text{expenses on credit}} \times 365$	Measures the number of days that it takes to pay suppliers. The denominator excludes non-cash expenses such as depreciation, as well as immediate cash outlays such as salaries and wages
Accounts aging analysis	Tracks the percentage of accounts payable that are current, 30 days overdue, 60 days overdue and more than 90 days overdue. This analysis can be a leading indicator of supplier issues

Accrued liabilities arise where your company has received goods or services, but they have not been invoiced or paid for. It's good business practice to have established procedures for month-end cutoffs and accrued liability recognition. This will help you in better understanding the amount of capital tied up in your company.

Other Working Capital Accounts

There can be a variety of other current assets, depending on the nature of your company. You should bear in mind that any current asset represents a capital investment in your company which should command a return. Many companies have the opportunity to reduce the amount of capital that they have tied up in prepaid expenses and deposits by analyzing the composition of those accounts more closely and deferring payment where possible. Some business owners and executives are astonished to discover that they may be entitled to recover certain prepaid expenses and deposits. They just need to ask!

Some companies have deferred revenues on account of billing for goods or services before they are delivered. As noted above, deferred revenues are a good thing, because they reduce the amount of capital tied up in your company. Where the invoices for those deferred revenues are paid prior to delivery, your customers have effectively financed your company at little or no cost.

Fixed Assets

Capital spending should be carefully managed in any company. You should classify capital expenditures as being required either to *sustain* your operations or *grow* your company. In some cases, a particular capital expenditure will comprise an element of both (e.g., the replacement of existing production equipment with higher capacity equipment).

Sustaining capital includes spending that is required to keep up to industry standards and to *maintain your company's competitive advantage*. Therefore, while the purchase of more modern equipment may improve product quality or employee safety, that expenditure would be classified as "sustaining" if it were needed in order to maintain existing revenue and profitability levels. Conversely, if improved product quality was expected to lead to higher revenues or lower costs, then it would be considered growth capital.

Remember that when estimating sustaining capital requirements, you need to take a long-term view, given that most capital assets will have to be replaced at some point. It's common for business owners and executives to underestimate their company's sustaining capital requirements over the long run, which can result in a misleading valuation conclusion. Examining capital expenditure requirements by fixed asset category can assist in ensuring a comprehensive review.

Where capital expenditures are classified as "growth", such growth should give rise to higher cash flow through lower costs (e.g., operating efficiencies) or increased revenue (e.g., higher capacity). In order to ensure that spending on growth capital is justified, you should conduct a *net present value analysis*, which measures the initial (after-tax) cost of the growth capital investment against the present value of the after-tax cash flow stream that the investment is expected to generate.

For example, assume that management of Tasty Snacks is considering the purchase of more efficient production equipment at a cost of $1 million. The equipment is expected to generate cost savings of $300,000 per year over its five-year useful life, growing by inflation at 2%. The equipment will be depreciated for tax purposes on a declining balance basis at a rate of 40% per year, with one-half of the depreciation allowed in the initial year. The equipment will be sold for its undepreciated tax value at the end of the fifth year. Tasty Snacks has a cost of capital of 13% and is subject to an income tax rate of 30%.

Exhibit 9H : Tasty Snacks Ltd. Net Present Value Analysis $(000)

				Year		
	Investment	1	2	3	4	5
Cost Savings		300	306	312	318	325
Tax impact		(90)	(92)	(94)	(96)	(97)
After-tax cost savings		210	214	218	223	227
Tax savings on depreciation		60	96	58	35	21
Acquisition/sale of equipment	(1,000)					104
Net cash flow	(1,000)	270	310	276	257	352
Net present value at 13%	19					
Tax Base of equipment						
Opening balance		1,000	800	480	288	173
Tax depreciation		(200)	(320)	(192)	(115)	(69)
Closing balance		800	480	288	173	104

This analysis shows a marginal benefit of $19,000 from the purchase of the equipment, meaning that the investment is essentially neutral to shareholder value. Therefore, management of Tasty Snacks should carefully consider other qualitative factors (e.g., health & safety, production disruption, etc.) prior to making a final decision.

Note in the example above that the equipment would be depreciated on a declining balance basis, which generates a greater benefit in the near term. This is common for many types of fixed assets. It's important to understand how the major capital assets in your company are treated for tax purposes. The tax authorities will often provide for an accelerated write-off of certain equipment in order to encourage companies to invest in productivity improvements.

Another useful metric to consider when evaluating capital expenditures is the payback period. Payback is a simple analysis that asks "how long will it take to get my money back from this investment?" While payback analysis ignores the cost of capital, it does help you to consider the risk associated with investments having a longer payback period. In the example above, the savings of $300,000 per year based on a $1 million investment results in a payback period of about 3.3 years, on a pre-tax basis.

Many companies capitalize smaller assets (rather than expensing them) in order to increase reported EBITDA. This practice is common in public companies, where accounting profit maximization is desired. However, this practice serves to erode shareholder value because the timing of the cash outlay is the same, but the associated tax benefit is delayed.

Some useful metrics for fixed asset management are as follows:

Exhibit 9I : Fixed Asset Ratios

Sustaining capital expenditures to EBITDA	Measures the degree to which cash from operations has to be reinvested in your company. Sustaining capital estimates are used as part of the multiple of EBITDA less Capex methodology (Chapter 2). Sustaining capital levels are also considered in the terminal value component of the DCF methodology (Chapter 3)
Total capital expenditures to revenues	Helps in assessing capital spending requirements from a macro perspective
Fixed Asset Efficiency Ratio $= \dfrac{\text{Revenues}}{\text{Net book value of fixed assets}}$	Helps in assessing the efficiency of fixed asset utilization
Capacity Utilization $= \dfrac{\text{Actual output}}{\text{Output capacity}}$	Measures actual output against the estimated capacity limit. Recall from Chapter 6 that using up available capacity can generate incremental revenues without significant incremental cost. It can also help in identifying underutilized assets, which could be sold for salvage value if not required. Remember that capacity utilization may be affected by seasonality

Lease vs. Buy

One discussion point that often arises in the context of fixed asset management is whether capital assets should be leased or purchased. Lease vs. buy is a financing decision, not an operating decision. It does not change the assets that are required to run your company, simply who owns those assets and how they are paid for.

Leasing assets can be attractive because it provides financial leverage (discussed in the next chapter). In addition, depending on the structure of the lease, it may be possible to write off lease payments in the period incurred, which offers a greater tax benefit than what is afforded by claiming tax depreciation on acquired assets. Many companies also look to operating leases as a means of providing off balance sheet financing (i.e., the benefits of using the asset without having to recognize the related liability on the balance sheet).

However, leasing can also have drawbacks. The interest rate embedded in lease payments can be high. Further, there may be covenants or restrictions imposed on your company as a condition to lease financing.

Key Points to Remember

- Working capital management can offer significant benefits in terms of higher shareholder value, so long as your company's cash flow and risk profile are not adversely affected.

- Ratio analysis can be helpful in managing working capital, but you need to be aware of the limitations.

- Send invoices out to customers promptly, or even in advance (to create deferred revenues) and follow-up rigorously with collection efforts.

- Classify capital expenditures between sustaining and growth, and ensure that growth spending will be accretive to shareholder value based on a net present value analysis.

- Lease vs. buy is a financing decision that requires consideration of both quantitative and qualitative factors.

10 Debt Financing

D ebt financing is a double-edged sword – what can help you can also hurt you. The use of debt within your company reduces the need for equity financing, and by extension increases shareholder returns. However, debt financing consumes cash to service interest expense and principal repayments. In addition, it increases the risk attached to your equity investment, since debt ranks ahead of equity against the assets and earnings power of your company. Therefore, a balance must be struck between the benefits of using debt on the one hand, and the cost and risk associated with debt on the other.

In Chapter 4, we discussed how to estimate a *normalized* amount of debt for the purpose of valuing your company. You may decide to use more or less than the estimated normalized amount, depending on your business operating philosophy and personal preferences. Remember that the enterprise value of your company is independent of how it's financed. However, the actual amount of debt outstanding is deducted from enterprise value to determine shareholder value. In this chapter we will address the factors that you should consider when deciding on the actual debt financing levels for your company.

The Magic of Financial Leverage

There tend to be two types of business owners and executives – those who love debt financing, and those who avoid it like the plague. Debt financing can help to increase shareholder returns, but at the expense of higher risk.

Consider the example of Tasty Snacks Ltd. The company generates $7.15 million of earnings before interest and taxes (EBIT, which in this case approximates pre-tax cash flow) and has a 30% income tax rate. If Tasty Snacks did not use any debt, it would require $40 million of tangible net worth in order to support its net operating assets. Rather, Tasty Snacks currently has $15 million of senior debt financing, at an interest rate of 6%, and the remaining $25 million has been financed by equity. You may also recall from Chapter 4 that management of Tasty Snacks estimated that the company's debt capacity was approximately $25 million, and that a "normalized" amount of debt financing was $20 million, in order to leave some cushion for unforeseen events. A comparison of the return on tangible net worth for Tasty Snacks at various levels of debt financing is as follows:

Exhibit 10A : Tasty Snacks Ltd. Impact of Debt Financing on Shareholder Returns $(000)

	Capital Structure Alternatives			
	Unlevered $0 Debt	Existing $15M Debt	Normalized $20M Debt	Capacity $25M Debt
Cash flow before interest and taxes	7,150	7,150	7,150	7,150
Interest expense	0	(900)	(1,200)	(1,500)
Cash flow before tax	7,150	6,250	5,950	5,650
Income taxes	(2,150)	(1,880)	(1,790)	(1,700)
Net cash flow	5,000	4,370	4,160	3,950
Capital Structure				
Debt	0	15,000	20,000	25,000
Equity (tangible net worth)	40,000	25,000	20,000	15,000
Total	40,000	40,000	40,000	40,000
Return on tangible net worth	12.5%	17.5%	20.8%	26.3%

By using $15 million of senior debt rather than all-equity financing (i.e., unlevered), Tasty Snacks has increased its return on tangible net worth from 12.5% to 17.5%. If management of Tasty Snacks believes that a normalized level of senior debt financing is $20 million, then the company can raise an additional $5 million in debt financing and increase its return on tangible net worth to almost 21%. The return on tangible net worth could exceed 26% if management levered the company to its senior debt capacity of $25 million. However, the cost of that higher potential return would be a significant increase in financial risk (discussed below), as well as the practical issues relating to more restrictive covenants.

By replacing equity with debt, the owner of Tasty Snacks, Mr. Goody can use some of the capital that is tied up in the company and invest that money elsewhere, thereby creating a more diversified portfolio for himself (and reducing risk). Therefore, the use of debt financing is often used in recapitalization strategies, as discussed in Chapter 13.

As an aside, note that the return on tangible net worth of 12.5% determined in Exhibit 10A is less than the unlevered cost of equity for Tasty Snacks of 15%, as set out in Chapter 4. The 15% unlevered rate of return on equity is a *market-driven* rate of return used to calculate the company's cost of capital. The return on tangible net worth measures actual returns against invested equity capital. It does not impact the cost of capital for Tasty Snacks.

It's important to remember that using debt does not impact the enterprise value of your company, because the determination of enterprise value is independent of how your company is financed. Enterprise value is based on what the market believes is a normalized level of debt in your company. You may decide to use more or less than the estimated normalized amount.

It follows that *using debt instead of equity to finance your company does not, in itself, create shareholder value.* However, the use of debt does affect the portion of enterprise value which remains with the shareholders of your company. While using debt can serve to increase the return on equity, the higher potential return is required in order to compensate for higher financial risk. Shareholder value is created where your company earns a return on invested capital in excess of its cost of capital. This point was illustrated in Chapter 6. Cost of capital is based on a normalized capital structure, which is market-driven.

Beware of Financial Risk

Debt financing is attractive because interest rates are relatively low. Furthermore, interest expense is tax deductible, so the government helps to finance your company. However, using debt in your company introduces additional risk, referred to as *financial risk*. Financial risk is over and above operating risk and arises because debt holders have a priority claim on the assets and cash flow of your company.

We'll dispense with the formula for calculating the specific financial risk premium for a given level of debt. However, you should recognize that the premium for financial risk increases exponentially as more debt is added into your company.

Using the example for Tasty Snacks, the *unlevered cost of equity* for the company was estimated at 15% (see Chapter 4). This denotes the starting point in the chart below. As more debt is substituted for equity, the financial risk premium, and hence the *levered cost of equity* (which incorporates both operating risk and financial risk), begins to rise dramatically.

Exhibit 10B : Tasty Snacks Ltd. Impact of Financial Leverage

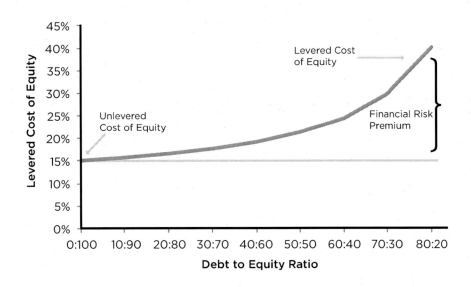

Even beyond the mathematical computation of financial risk, too much leverage within your company can create other issues, such as the time and effort needed to manage your banker and the loss of flexibility due to restrictive covenants. In addition to formal bank covenants, excessive debt can lead to practical challenges in your company, such as limiting the amount of capital available to finance growth, in favour of having to make debt payments. Remember that it's easier to raise debt where your company has a good equity base, rather than trying to raise equity to reduce excessive debt within your company.

How Much Debt is Right for Your Company?

Academics love to debate the subject of capital structure – i.e., the extent to which a company should be financed by debt vs. equity. As noted in Chapter 4, the ideal capital structure is where the weighted average cost of capital for your company is minimized through balancing the benefits of low-cost debt financing against the risks of using debt. However, there is no magic formula that can be used to determine precisely how much debt you should have in your company. It's both an economic decision and a personal decision, and you will have to live within your comfort zone. But here are a few things to consider:

- the cost of debt, both in terms of the stated interest rate, as well as other fees and costs (e.g., standby charges and loan arrangement fees);

- the availability of debt, which is tied to economic cycles. This extends to the type of debt that is available (senior, subordinated or mezzanine), which is discussed later in this chapter;

- whether or not personal or inter-corporate guarantees are required;

- the type and amount of assets within your company that can be offered as security;

- the level and stability of cash flows that can be used to service interest expense and principal repayments;

- industry norms; debt levels and capital structures can vary widely, even for companies operating within the same industry. However, where your company has higher amounts of debt than industry norms, it may cause the market to believe that you are over-levered, thereby making it more difficult to raise incremental debt;

- a normalized capital structure, as set out in Chapter 4. Similar to industry norms, higher debt than normal can have negative implications where market participants believe that your company is over-levered. By the same token, using significantly less debt than a normalized amount may be viewed as being too conservative;

- the covenants that your company will have to operate within. This is a very important consideration, since it could impede growth plans for your company or limit your ability to make dividend payments or other distributions;

- the terms of repayment, and whether there are any penalties for prepayment; and

- future plans for your company and the likely funding requirements at that time. In this regard, many business owners and executives like to raise debt instead of equity in order to avoid dilution of the existing ownership interests. However, if additional funding will be required in the future, it's easier to secure debt financing on reasonable terms when you have a strong equity base within your company, rather than trying to raise equity on reasonable terms where your company has too much debt.

Exhibit 10C : Factors to Consider When Raising Debt

- Cost of debt

- Availability of debt

- Need for guarantees

- Underlying assets

- Level and stability of cash flows

- Industry norms

- Normalized debt levels

- Restrictive covenants

- Terms of repayment

- Future plans and related financing

As noted in Chapter 4, the amount of senior debt that a bank may be willing to lend your company will be based on its assessment of your cash flows and assets. It's generally wise not to over-leverage your company, and to leave a bit of a cushion just in case things don't turn out as planned. Remember that the more time you spend managing your banker, the less time that you have to manage your company.

What Type of Debt Should You Raise?

Senior Debt Financing

Senior debt financing refers to debt that ranks ahead of other creditors in terms of its claim on your company's assets. In most cases, it is secured by specific assets (e.g., accounts receivable, inventory or equipment), and is sometimes referred to as asset-based lending. Senior debt lenders tend to have a risk-adverse mentality since they are at risk of experiencing losses but are not rewarded for potential gains that a shareholder would enjoy. They tend to prefer companies with quality assets (e.g., accounts receivable from large customers, saleable inventories and real property) and that generate stable cash flows.

Senior debt lenders will stipulate a maximum amount of financing based on your company's underlying assets, as well as its cash flow generating capability. In the current economic environment, senior debt capacity often falls in the range from 1.5x to 3.0x EBITDA, depending on the quality of the cash flow (e.g., the degree of volatility and the need for capital reinvestment) and the underlying assets securing the debt. Asset coverage ratios were discussed in Chapter 4.

Senior debt lenders usually will require that your company operate within the limits of certain financial ratios, such as:

- the current ratio (current assets divided by current liabilities);

- debt to tangible net worth (total liabilities divided by tangible net worth);

- debt serviceability ratios, such as total funded debt to EBITDA; and

- asset coverage ratios, such as those relating to the value of accounts receivable, inventories and fixed assets (see Chapter 4).

Your company would also be subject to other covenants and restrictions, such as those involving capital spending, dividend payments and the sale of assets, as well as financial reporting requirements. Depending on their nature, these covenants and restrictions can be quite onerous.

Subordinated Debt and Mezzanine Financing

Subordinated debt ranks behind senior debt in its claim against your company's assets. Mezzanine financing refers to financing that takes on characteristics of both subordinated debt and equity.

Like senior debt, subordinated debt and mezzanine financing bind your company with a legal obligation to repay the principal amount. However, repayment terms can vary considerably, and sometimes are structured with *balloon payments* whereby the entire principal amount is repayable at the end of the loan term.

In the current economic environment, and depending on a company's credit rating, it's not uncommon for subordinated debt lenders to seek a coupon rate in the order of 10%, compared to senior debt with rates in the order of 5%. Mezzanine financiers usually seek total rates of return in the range of 15% to 20% (given the higher risk profile), which may be comprised of a cash coupon rate, payment in kind (PIK) interest (i.e., deferred interest payments) and some form of equity participation, such as warrants or a conversion feature. The amount of subordinated debt or mezzanine financing that a company can secure usually is in the range of 1.0x to 1.5x EBITDA, over and above senior debt lending.

While the cost of subordinated debt and mezzanine financing is considerably more expensive than senior debt, it's generally less expensive than equity financing (on a levered basis), particularly when you consider that interest expense is tax deductible.

Long-Term Debt vs. Short-Term Debt

Another consideration is whether to secure long-term debt or short-term operating debt (e.g., a bank line of credit). While short-term debt tends to be less expensive, long-term debt affords greater stability in financing. Short-term debt usually bears a floating interest rate of prime plus a specified premium, often in the order of 0.25% to 3.0%, depending on the amount and quality of security. The interest rate on long-term debt tends to be higher.

As a general rule, you should follow the *matching principle* for debt financing. That is, long-term assets (e.g., fixed assets and corporate acquisitions) should be financed with long-term debt, such as term loans, mortgages and capital leases. Conversely, short-term assets (such as accounts receivable) are usually financed with short-term debt, such as a bank operating loan, which allows the short-term debt to fluctuate as needed.

Key Points to Remember

- While the use of debt within your company can increase equity returns and allows individual shareholders to diversify their economic risk, it does not, in itself, create shareholder value.

- Beware of the implications of financial risk, which increases exponentially as more debt is added into your company.

- The amount of senior debt that your company can raise is a function of its cash flows and underlying assets, but you must beware of the related covenants which may be quite onerous.

- Subordinated debt and mezzanine financing can be costly, but they are cheaper than pure equity financing on an after-tax basis.

- Use the matching principle when considering whether to raise short-term debt or long-term debt.

CHAPTER

11 Equity Financing

Equity financing is preferable to debt financing where your company is looking to strengthen its balance sheet. In other cases, equity financing may be necessary because debt financing is either not available or not practical. Where the existing shareholders are unwilling or unable to provide the necessary equity financing themselves, then your company has to look externally. A public offering can be used if your company is already public, or if it is a private company that is looking to become public. However, for both private companies and public companies, private equity financing can also be an attractive alternative.

One of the obvious questions that comes to mind for existing shareholders when raising equity is: "What percentage of ownership will I have to give up?" In the context of a privately-held company, the existing shareholders should not only consider the issue of dilution, but also the terms of the equity investment, which includes the provisions of a shareholders' agreement. Similar to raising debt financing, raising equity does not in itself create shareholder value. Rather, shareholder value is created when your company earns a return on invested capital that exceeds its cost of capital.

In this chapter, we'll address private equity financing from the perspective of supporting your company's growth initiatives. Private equity in the context of a financial buyer for your company, or helping to facilitate a management buy-out, is addressed in Part III. In this chapter, we will also discuss the pros and cons of a public offering as well as employee share ownership plans and shareholders' agreements.

Private Equity Financing

A private equity firm is an organization that looks to generate a return on its equity investments in public and/or private companies. There is a wide array of organizations that call themselves private equity firms, ranging from groups of wealthy individuals who pool together a few hundred thousand dollars, to divisions of major pension funds with billions in capital. But the one thing that private equity firms have in common is that they all want to invest in companies with the intention of exiting the investment at some point, and generate a significant return on their capital.

Private equity can be an attractive source of financing to assist your company in many initiatives, including financing expansion plans, recapitalizations, divisional spin-offs and management buyouts.

Investment Criteria

The investment criteria used by private equity firms can range considerably. Some of the most common parameters include the following:

- **minority or control positions.** Some private equity firms will only invest in a company if they can have a controlling interest. Other private equity firms will consider non-controlling (i.e., minority) interests. However, the provisions of the shareholders' agreement may provide certain veto powers or "negative control" to those firms with a minority interest;

- **investment size (or "bite size").** Most private equity firms have a minimum and maximum amount that they will invest in a company. Because of the time and effort required to consummate and manage an investment, there tends to be a greater number of private equity firms interested in larger size deals ($10 million investment size or greater) than smaller deals;

- **industry specialization.** Some private equity firms specialize in one or more industry segments that they believe will provide attractive returns. Industry specialization also helps the private equity firm to better understand the dynamics of those industries, which can help them be more effective in managing their portfolio investments and in devising an exit strategy;

- **life cycle stage.** Some private equity firms will focus on companies that are in an early stage of their life cycle, or even start-up or pre-revenue companies. These private equity firms are commonly referred to as *venture capital* investors. Other private equity firms prefer more mature and established companies; and

- **geographic area.** Many smaller private equity firms will invest only in a particular region in order to ensure that they can be physically close to their investments.

Most private equity firms publicize their investment criteria and their investment portfolio on their website, which can help you to determine whether a particular private equity firm may be a fit for your company.

When a private equity firm invests in a private company, it will insist on having a shareholders' agreement. Even where the private equity firm holds a minority stake in a company, it typically will require that the shareholders' agreement set out certain major decisions for which the private equity firm has a veto right (e.g., sale of the company, significant capital expenditures, capital injections).

The provisions dealing with shareholder liquidity are important as well. In most cases, the individual shareholders are restricted in their ability to dispose of their shares outside of a liquidity event for all shareholders. There are some exceptions (such as death, disability and termination), but in many cases these early exits result in a discount from fair value. Various provisions commonly found within a shareholders' agreement are discussed later in this chapter.

Once a private equity firm is satisfied that the proposed investment meets its criteria, it will gauge the merits of the investment on the following considerations:

- the quality of the company. Private equity firms usually look to invest in companies that have a sustainable competitive advantage and/or a defendable market position. Companies that are leaders within a market niche are often viewed as particularly attractive;

- the strength of the company's management team. Private equity firms seldom get involved in the day-to-day operations of a company (although some are more involved than others). Rather, they typically prefer to have one or more seats on the Board of Directors (depending on the size and type of investment) and to rely on the management team to execute the growth strategy. Therefore, the private equity firm looks for a management team with the right set of capabilities and a proven track record;

- the quality of the business case underlying the growth initiatives for which financing is being sought. In this regard, private equity firms will assess the plausibility of achieving the forecast results and the risks relating thereto; and

- the time horizon. Private equity firms will not invest in a company where they do not believe there is a viable exit at some point. That exit may be in the form of selling the entire company to a strategic buyer, an initial public offering or being bought out by other shareholders. The target investment horizon for an exit can vary significantly. Some private equity investors are more patient than others. Most private equity firms look for an exit within a three to seven year time frame. Some larger firms, such as pension funds, have longer time horizons.

Some private equity firms will look to directly invest in common shares. Others will structure their investment differently in order to create equity type returns. For example, some private equity firms use mezzanine debt financing with warrants, while others will use convertible debt or convertible preferred shares.

Private equity firms will develop financial models to determine whether their rate of return criteria will be met. While targeted rates of return vary, it is not uncommon for private equity firms to have target rates of return on equity in the range of 25% to 30% when investing in established companies. These represent *levered* rates of return on equity, which incorporate both operating risk and financial risk. Higher rates of return (40% +) are common targets for early stage companies.

Selecting the Right Private Equity Firm

Private equity financing should not be viewed as a one-way street. You should expect to receive more from a private equity firm than just a lump sum of cash. Other important considerations include:

- the ability of the private equity firm to accommodate follow-on financing (commonly referred to as "dry powder") that may be needed to support future growth initiatives or an unexpected shortfall in cash flow;

- alignment of interests with your company's executive team in terms of investment horizon, growth strategies, participation in upside potential (e.g., through an employee share ownership plan (ESOP)) and the private equity firm's level of patience or tolerance for shortfalls from plan; and

- value-added service offerings. Private equity firms should be expected to provide things such as strategic advice, customer contacts, best practices and other assistance that help your company to grow and prosper, particularly where the private equity firm has current or past investments in the same industry.

Challenges with Private Equity Financing

Having a private equity firm as a partner introduces a number of challenges. Private equity firms:

- given their investment time horizon, tend to focus on short-term results. This can place considerable pressure on management;

- will often encourage the use of debt financing within your company to leverage their equity returns. Therefore, you may have to manage your company with greater financial risk and more restrictive covenants;

- will exercise their influence through participation on your company's Board of Directors. Therefore, you may need to adopt a more formalized governance structure than you may have been accustomed to;

- usually have additional reporting requirements, such as more detailed periodic financial statements, as well as management and board presentations. Such requirements can represent a significant change from the way your company operated in the past, and may prove onerous for management; and

- may have fees and costs. Many private equity firms charge their portfolio companies placement fees or other fees when making an investment. These costs can be significant. In addition, your company may have to incur legal expenses on its own behalf and reimburse those incurred by the private equity firm.

Initial Public Offerings (IPOs)

For companies of a sufficient size, an IPO can be an attractive means of providing growth financing. Smaller companies with an attractive growth story have also used IPOs as a means of raising capital. While an IPO can also provide liquidity for existing shareholders, market participants tend to have greater interest where the capital is being raised for the purpose of funding a company's growth initiatives, as opposed to an exit strategy for the current owners. In some cases, an IPO is a combination of both.

There are numerous benefits to being a public company, which can be summarized as follows:

- the public equity markets often provide valuation multiples that are beyond what a company could obtain through private equity financing or other sources of equity;

- further to the above point, higher valuation multiples can result in a lower cost of equity financing and, by extension, a lower cost of capital;

- once a company is public, it becomes easier to return to the equity markets to raise additional financing (a public offering or private placement);

- public companies can more easily offer stock incentives as a means of attracting and retaining key employees;

- existing shareholders have a forum for ongoing liquidity, subject to certain trading restrictions and disclosure requirements;

- public companies sometimes benefit from a higher profile and greater prestige than private companies; and

- public companies can more easily consummate acquisitions through a share exchange and, in effect, use their shares as currency.

However, there are numerous risks and drawbacks of being of public company that must be carefully considered. Among the most notable are the following:

- the costs involved in launching an IPO are significant, including legal and audit costs, investment banking fees and so on;

- the ongoing governance and compliance costs and management time required to remain a public company can also be quite hefty. In effect, these costs make it very difficult for smaller companies to become public or to remain public. Consequently, many smaller public companies have privatized in recent years;

- the ongoing disclosure requirements and loss of confidentiality;

- shareholders of public companies will often emphasize short-term accounting results, such as earnings per share, which may not be consistent with building shareholder value over the longer term;

- further to the previous point, public companies often experience pressure from institutional shareholders and are exposed to the risk that significant shareholders will elect someone to the Board of Directors who will operate with a self-interested agenda;

- public companies can become hostile takeover targets. While poison pills and other mechanism can be used to help defend against that possibility, the use of such tactics is coming under increased scrutiny from a corporate governance perspective;

- there are costs and challenges of having to deal with nuisance shareholders, even those with a relatively minor stake in the company; and

- smaller public companies often have issues relating to the liquidity of their shares, particularly where they are unable to obtain ongoing coverage from stock analysts. Consequently, shareholders may experience an *illiquidity discount*, and significant shareholders may not be able to liquidate their interest on attractive terms (thus becoming "stuckholders").

Exhibit 11A : Pros and Cons of Being a Public Company

Pros	Cons
Possible higher valuation multiples	Costs to launch an IPO
Lower cost of capital	Governance and compliance costs
Access to additional equity financing	Loss of confidentiality
Liquidity for shareholders	Emphasis on short-term accounting profit
Profile and prestige	Pressure from institutional shareholders
Acquisitions through share exchanges	Possible takeover target
	Nuisance shareholders
	Liquidity issues for smaller companies

Primary vs. Secondary Share Offerings

When raising equity capital, it's important to distinguish between a *primary share offering* and a *secondary share offering*. Simply put, a primary share offering sees money going into the company (and increasing its shareholder value), whereas a secondary share offering is a transaction between shareholders, and does not impact the shareholder value of the company itself.

Continuing with our example of Tasty Snacks, the company generates EBITDA of $10 million and has a valuation multiple of 5x, for an enterprise value of $50 million. The capital structure of the company currently consists of $15 million in debt and the balance in equity. Tasty Snacks is considering the purchase of another company, Yummy Treats Inc., for a price of $25 million. Tasty Snacks can raise an additional $15 million in debt, but will require $10 million in equity. Therefore, it approaches a private equity firm to fill the gap.

Exhibit 11B : Tasty Snacks Ltd. Primary Offering to Support Acquisition of Yummy Treats $(000)

	Existing Business	Acquisition	Pro Forma
Enterprise Value	50,000	25,000	75,000
Financed by:			
Debt	15,000	15,000	30,000
Equity	35,000	10,000	45,000
	50,000	25,000	75,000
Shareholder Value			
Existing Owner	35,000		35,000
Private Equity Firm		10,000	10,000
			45,000
Shareholders' Interest			
Existing Owner			78%
Private Equity Firm			22%
			100%

The net result is that following its investment, the private equity firm will own 22% of Tasty Snacks' equity, and the existing shareholder (Mr. Goody) will own the remaining 78%. In this case, the private equity firm participated in a primary share offering, where new shares were issued from treasury.

Had Mr. Goody used the acquisition opportunity to "take chips off the table" in the amount of $10 million, as well as fund the acquisition, then the transaction structure and the pro forma ownership of Tasty Snacks would be as follows:

Exhibit 11C : Tasty Snacks Ltd. Combined Primary and Secondary Offering $(000)

	Existing Business	Acquisition	Pro Forma
Enterprise Value	50,000	25,000	75,000
Financed by:			
Debt	15,000	15,000	30,000
Equity	35,000	10,000	45,000
	50,000	25,000	75,000
Shareholder Value			
Existing Owner	35,000	(10,000)	25,000
Private Equity Firm		20,000	20,000
			45,000
Shareholders' Interest			
Existing Owner			56%
Private Equity Firm			44%
			100%

Note that the pro forma equity value of Tasty Snacks remains at $45 million following the acquisition, but the ownership structure has now changed because of the secondary offering component.

Employee Share Ownership Plans (ESOPs)

Many business owners and executives of privately-held companies consider implementing an ESOP as a means of attracting, retaining and motivating employees. ESOPs can also be a means of raising equity capital among existing employees, but this tends to be a secondary objective since the amounts invested are usually relatively small.

While the benefits of a properly structured ESOP can be significant, including creating a culture that is conducive to building shareholder value, there are potential risks and issues that should be carefully considered before they are introduced.

In essence, an ESOP is an arrangement whereby certain employees of a company can become shareholders if they meet the specified criteria. Qualifying employees are either granted shares or an option to buy shares in a company at a specified price. The acquired shares usually are held until the employee leaves the company or a liquidity event occurs, such as a sale of the company to a strategic buyer or an initial public offering.

There is a considerable amount of flexibility in how an ESOP is designed. The first issue to be addressed when designing an ESOP is to determine the criteria for participation. In this regard, there are two basic schools of thought. The first alternative is to restrict ESOP participation to a handful of key employees. This can be a way of recognizing and incentivizing select individuals who are viewed as critical to the long-term success of the company, and making those individuals feel distinguished within the company. However, it can also lead to the creation of two classes of employees within a company – those that are ESOP-eligible and those who are not.

The other alternative is to extend the ESOP to all employees that meet certain basic criteria, such as having been employed with the company for a specified period of time. In this case, the magnitude of an employee's participation in the ESOP program often varies based on factors such as job title and compensation, so that senior managers are rewarded more than individuals who occupy administrative and junior positions. This approach allows for the benefits of the ESOP to be widespread, but requires a larger pool of shares to be made available, thereby diluting the interests of existing owners. A company-wide ESOP can also be more costly and time consuming to administer.

Another key consideration when designing the ESOP is to determine the size of the ESOP pool. That is to say, what proportion of ownership are the existing shareholders prepared to give up in favour of ESOP participants? The obvious trade-off is that a greater degree of ownership participation creates added incentive, but existing shareholders experience greater ownership dilution. Business owners and executives should also remember that an ESOP pool will grow over time, as new shares are issued. Therefore, if shares representing 4% of the company are issued pursuant to an ESOP each year, then the existing shareholders will have diluted their interest by 20% within a 5-year period. At that point, it may be difficult to modify the ESOP to slow down the rate of dilution, as employees will have established expectations.

It's also necessary to consider whether the ESOP will take the form of shares or options that can be exercised for shares. Other considerations are whether shares will be gifted to employees, or whether employees must acquire the shares at their prevailing fair market value. Requiring employees to acquire shares can be difficult for those individuals with limited financial resources – even if extended payment terms are offered. Options are attractive because the price paid for the shares (as determined pursuant to strike price of the option) usually takes place concurrently with a liquidity event, so the employee is not out-of-pocket. However, if the value of the shares declines, then the options may be "under water" and provide little incentive. Having employees actually own shares can help to solidify retention, since they will have made a monetary commitment. Some ESOPs are designed to include both an element of shares and options in order to balance the pros and cons of each alternative.

Establishing the characteristics of the ESOP shares is another key decision. In some cases, the shares issued pursuant to an ESOP have different rights and privileges than those held by the existing shareholders. For example, ESOP shares may be non-voting or have limited voting rights. While this can help to ensure that the existing owners retain voting control in the company, it can make employees feel as though they are receiving less economic value. Where the ESOP shares do have voting rights, it's important to consider whether and how ESOP participants will be represented on the company's Board of Directors. A properly structured shareholders' agreement is a critical component of any ESOP.

Finally, the provisions and restrictions governing the liquidity of the ESOP shares must be clearly established. In most cases, the shares received pursuant to an ESOP cannot be freely traded, and employees must wait for a "liquidity event" in order to get paid for their shares.

Where the liquidity event involves a sale of the company to a strategic buyer or an initial public offering, then payment for the ESOP shares is a non-issue, since external financing is available. However, liquidity events are more problematic when the company must finance the purchase of its own ESOP shares, such as when an employee quits or is terminated (most privately-held companies do not want former employees holding shares). In this regard, many ESOPs are designed such that, in the event of a voluntary departure from the company, the redemption price is subject to a discount from what their value may otherwise be. This serves as a type of penalty to an employee who leaves the company and wants to cash in.

Exhibit 11D : ESOP Considerations

- Eligibility for participation
- Size of the ESOP pool
- Shares vs. options
- Price for the shares
- Voting characteristics
- Liquidation opportunities and terms

Benefits and Drawbacks of an ESOP

The major benefits of an ESOP include:

- attracting, retaining and motivating key employees. This makes ESOPs particularly attractive in industries where specialized skills or knowledge are essential (such as technology);

- controlling the amount of cash compensation paid to employees, which can be critical for smaller and rapidly growing companies that need to preserve cash in order to finance growth initiatives;

- aligning the interests of employees with those of the business owners. A properly structured ESOP can encourage employees to think like entrepreneurs, and find new ways to grow the company and reduce costs. In particular, an ESOP can help to alleviate employee concerns about a liquidity event that involves a sale of the company to a strategic buyer, since the employees stand to benefit financially;

- attracting financing. Many commercial lenders and private equity firms perceive that there is less risk in dealing with a company that has a well-designed ESOP, since it can help ensure that key employees are committed to the company. This is particularly the case where employees must pay for shares on their issuance (rather than receiving options) since equity injections will help to strengthen the company's balance sheet; and

- creating income tax efficiency. Properly structured, employees participating in an ESOP will only be taxed on the disposition of their shares at capital gains rates, which is more attractive than salary income.

There are, however, issues, risks and costs that business owners and executives need to consider prior to implementing an ESOP in their company. Some of the most notable include:

- the up-front legal, administrative and accounting costs relating to developing and implementing the plan. Once the ESOP is established, there are additional ongoing costs in terms of financial reporting and valuation;

- additional governance requirements. Participants in an ESOP have certain rights as current or prospective shareholders within an organization. There may be a need for a formal board of directors where ESOP participants have representation. This may have an impact on the company's strategy and key decisions. Further, an ESOP will reduce the flexibility that business owners have in terms of making discretionary payments such as bonuses to themselves and family members;

- potential erosion of the company's cash reserves. As noted above, where employees leave the company, the shares that they received pursuant to the ESOP usually are redeemed. Even where the redemption price is subject to a discount, the company must still finance the redemption with other internal resources. As an alternative to a redemption discount (or in addition to one), some companies pay for redeemed shares over a period of several years (normally without interest) in order to alleviate financing issues;

- the possible de-motivating impact where share values have declined. Many companies experienced this phenomenon around 2009 with the downturn in economic conditions. Employees who acquired shares pursuant to an ESOP may have felt that they were forced to overpay. Where options were granted in lieu of shares, the strike price of those options may be so far "under water" that they provide little economic incentive; and

- possible friction among employees where not everyone participates in the ESOP. As noted above, this can create the perception of two classes of employees within an organization.

Exhibit 11E : Pros and Cons of an ESOP

Pros	Cons
Attract, retain, motivate employees	Initial and ongoing costs
Controlling cash compensation	Additional governance requirements
Alignment of interests with owners	Cash requirements for redemption
Attracting financing	Possible de-motivation if value declines
Income tax efficiency	Friction among classes of employees

In the end, business owners and executives who are considering an ESOP are well advised to do their homework and to get sound and objective professional advice. They must be satisfied that the prospective benefits will outweigh the costs involved. Further, as much as the legal and administration costs of an ESOP can be significant, the potential consequences of a poorly-designed ESOP can be far worse. It's much easier to implement an ESOP than to try to modify or cancel it afterwards. Hence the need to invest the time, effort and cost to ensure that an ESOP is designed properly from the start, and that the long-term implications of an ESOP are carefully considered.

Shareholders' Agreements

Over the years, I have advised numerous business owners and executives in situations involving a shareholder dispute within their company. The vast majority of those situations can be traced back to an inadequate or non-existent shareholders' agreement.

Shareholders' agreements establish the rights, privileges and obligations of the majority and minority shareholders. While not necessarily an initiative that creates shareholder value, the absence of an adequate shareholders' agreement can quickly result in the erosion of value that has been created. Shareholders' agreements should be drafted with the mindset that they will be used in the context of possible litigation. Therefore, it's worth the time, effort and money to get it right.

Shareholders' agreements should be in place wherever there is more than one owner in a private company, including family businesses, employee share ownership plans (ESOPs), joint ventures or private equity investors. Public companies can also make use of shareholders' agreements in the context of their investment in a non-public entity.

The major provisions of a shareholders' agreement are those dealing with decision making, triggering events, valuation and other circumstances that could lead to a transaction among the existing shareholders of a company.

Decision Making

The shareholders' agreement should clearly establish how decisions will be made within your company. It should specify the number of positions on the Board and the rights of shareholders to appoint Board members. While individual shareholders often will want to appoint themselves to the Board, it's good business practice where the Board has meaningful independent (i.e., non-shareholder) representation.

The shareholders' agreement should set out how decisions by the Board of Directors are to be made (e.g., simple majority, two-thirds majority, unanimous). It should also establish decisions that require shareholder approval, such as the sale or liquidation of the company, and the threshold for such approval. It can be dangerous to require unanimous shareholder approval of major decisions, given that it allows a shareholder with a relatively small ownership interest to thwart the intentions of the majority.

Triggering Events

A triggering event is one that gives rise to the right or the obligation for a shareholder to buy or sell an equity interest in your company. The triggering events that should be addressed in a shareholders' agreement (sometimes referred to as the 5 Ds) are:

- **Death** of an individual shareholder or a change in control of a corporate shareholder;

- **Disability** – referring to a long-term or permanent disability that would prohibit an individual shareholder from being involved in your company;

- **Departure** – either voluntarily or by way of termination;

- **Divorce** – given that, in the context of family law entitlements, shareholders may want the right to buy out another shareholder going through divorce proceedings, rather than have the shares owned by that individual's spouse; and

- **Debt** – referring to the bankruptcy of an individual or corporate shareholder.

Properly structured, a shareholders' agreement can ensure that for a shareholder who is terminating their association with your company, there will be a market for their shares at a price that all shareholders believe to be fair. It also provides continuing shareholders with control over outside parties becoming shareholders.

For each triggering event, the shareholders' agreement should set out how the transaction is to be effected (i.e., purchase of shares by the other shareholders, or by the company and subsequently cancelled), the method of determining the transaction price, and the terms of payment. In this regard, different triggering events can give rise to different valuation provisions or payment terms. For example, the valuation provisions or payment terms sometimes are less favourable to a shareholder who voluntarily withdraws from the company, as contrasted to the provisions governing death (which may be financed through life insurance proceeds).

Valuation Provisions

Shareholders' agreements sometimes specify how fair market value (or some other definition of value) is to be determined in the context of a transaction pursuant to a triggering event. The most common methods for establishing value are:
   (i) agreement by the shareholders;
   (ii) pre-determined formula;
   (iii) independent expert;
   (iv) arbitration; or
   (v) a combination of the latter two where there is disagreement among experts.

Where valuation formulas are used, they often are based on some predetermined multiple of historical accounting earnings, cash flow (e.g., EBITDA) or book value. The use of pre-determined formulas may result in inequities for several reasons. In particular, the value of your company is influenced by both internal and external factors, and a pre-determined formula does not reflect such changes over time.

Frequently, the provisions of a shareholders' agreement pertaining to the valuation of a particular equity interest are inadequate. General terms such as *fair market value* are not sufficiently clear, and leave open the possibility of differences in interpretation that can materially affect the derived value of a particular equity interest. Therefore, it's important that the shareholders' agreement clearly define how value is to be determined for each triggering event. In particular, the shareholders' agreement normally should address at least the following with respect to value:

- whether the "en bloc" shareholder value of your company should be determined on an *intrinsic* (i.e., "stand-alone") basis, or whether so-called *special interest purchasers* should be taken into account. A special interest purchaser is one that believes it can realize post-acquisition synergies by combining the acquired company with its existing operations, and therefore may be willing to pay a premium (i.e., strategic value) over the intrinsic value of a company. As a practical matter, in the absence of open market negotiations, the quantification of post-acquisition synergies is highly speculative, and intrinsic value normally is adopted as the appropriate value term; and

- whether or not a *minority discount* should apply. As discussed in Chapter 1, a minority discount is a reduction from the pro rata portion of "en bloc" fair market value that sometimes is applied to a minority interest given that a minority shareholder cannot unilaterally control the company. For example, if the total shareholder value of Tasty Snacks Ltd. is $35 million, it does not necessarily follow that a 10% equity interest in that company is worth $3.5 million. In some cases, a minority interest may be worth significantly less than its pro rata value, depending on the circumstances. However, shareholders' agreements often specify that a particular equity interest is to be valued as a pro rata portion of en bloc fair market value without the application of a discount for non-control, illiquidity or otherwise (commonly referred to as *fair value*).

Buy/Sell Provisions

In addition to the triggering events discussed above, shareholders' agreements often provide one or more shareholders with the right, or the obligation, to put (sell) their shares to the other shareholder(s), or to call (buy) the interest of the other shareholder(s). Similar to other triggering events, a put or call option may provide that the transaction is to be effected at a pre-established price, a pre-determined formula, by independent expert, or arbitration when it's exercised.

A shareholders' agreement may also provide for reciprocal buy/sell provisions, often called a *shotgun* clause. Shotgun clauses most often are encountered in situations involving two equal (50/50) shareholders, and provide that one shareholder can offer to sell his or her shares to the other shareholder at a price and on terms specified in the offer. The shareholder receiving the offer must either:

- accept the offer, and acquire the shares of the offering shareholder at the price and terms specified in the offer; or

- reject the offer, which requires the shareholder receiving the offer to sell his or her shares to the offering shareholder at the price and terms specified in the offer.

Whichever course of action is adopted by the shareholder receiving the offer, it results in a binding agreement of purchase and sale between the shareholders. Assuming the shareholders are of relatively equal negotiating strength, a shotgun clause tends to ensure the liquidity of each shareholder's interest. Consequently, it establishes what the parties believe to be a fair price for the shares.

Issues may arise in a shotgun clause where the shareholders have materially different negotiating strength. This includes situations where one of the shareholders has access to greater financial resources, or where only one of the shareholders is actively involved in your company, and therefore is more knowledgeable about its operations and future prospects. In some circumstances, particularly in the case of small companies, one shareholder may enjoy *personal goodwill*. Recall from Chapter 6 that personal goodwill refers to the benefit that accrues to the company by virtue of the good name, reputation, knowledge and so on, of a particular individual, and it's not transferable. Accordingly, the company may be worth considerably more to a shareholder that has personal goodwill compared to a shareholder that does not.

Right of First Refusal and Right of First Offer

Shareholders' agreements often include *right of first refusal* provisions. Among other things, these provisions allow continuing shareholders to accept or reject proposed new shareholders. Pursuant to a right of first refusal, the shareholder wishing to sell solicits third party offers. The shareholder(s) holding the right of first refusal is then presented with the best third party offer received and is given the opportunity to purchase the selling shareholder's interest based on the price and terms of that offer. If the continuing shareholder elects not to purchase the shares within an agreed period of time, the selling shareholder can then sell their interest to the party making the offer on those same terms.

As an alternative to a right of first refusal, some shareholders' agreements contain a *right of first offer*, whereby a shareholder wishing to sell their interest establishes the price and terms of sale, which is presented to the shareholder(s) holding the first offer right. If the shareholder(s) having the right of first offer elects not to acquire the shares within an agreed time period, the selling shareholder is free to sell their interest in the open market at a price and on terms that are not less favourable to the seller than what was offered to the other shareholder(s).

The right of first refusal is preferable from the point of view of the shareholder holding the refusal right. Third party purchasers often are reluctant to spend a significant amount of time assessing a potential share acquisition in the face of an overriding right of first refusal. The right of first offer is better from the seller's perspective. Although it forces the prospective seller to be disciplined when establishing the initial price and terms offered to the shareholder(s) holding the first offer right, in the event the offer is not accepted, the seller is able to deal with third party purchasers unencumbered by a first refusal right.

Drag Along and Tag Along Provisions

Many acquirers of privately-held company shares will close a transaction only if 100% share ownership is delivered. In such circumstances, the controlling shareholder will not want to have a transaction thwarted by one or more minority shareholders. Therefore, shareholders' agreements frequently provide that if an offer is received for all of the outstanding shares that is acceptable to a specified majority of the shareholders, then all shareholders are obliged to tender to the offer on the same terms and conditions. These *drag along* provisions protect the liquidity of a controlling shareholder or a group of shareholders that represent control.

At the same time, a shareholders' agreement should ensure minority shareholders the opportunity to sell into a third party offer at the same price and terms as accepted by the majority. These *tag along* provisions (or *coattail* provisions) protect the liquidity of all shareholders in the event of such an offer.

Participation in a Subsequent Sale

In some cases where a shareholder disposes of his or her interest to other shareholders of the company, the acquiring shareholder(s) realizes a windfall profit shortly thereafter pursuant to a subsequent sale of the company to a third party acquirer. To alleviate such perceived unfairness, shareholders' agreements sometimes provide that during a specified time period after the departing shareholder disposes of their interest, that shareholder is entitled to participate in any gain on a subsequent sale of the company to a third party.

Exhibit 11F : Major Provisions in Shareholders' Agreements

- Decision making
- Triggering events
- Valuation
- Buy/Sell
- Right of first refusal (first offer)
- Drag along/tag along
- Participation in a subsequent sale

Key Points to Remember

- In order to attract private equity financing, your company needs to have a competitive advantage, a good growth story, a strong management team and a viable exit strategy.

- Going public can appear attractive, but is fraught with challenges, including the costs involved, loss of confidentiality, additional governance requirements and possible liquidity issues.

- The amount of equity given up by existing shareholders when raising equity capital will depend on whether the transaction represents a primary or a secondary share offering.

- ESOPs can be an attractive mechanism for attracting, retaining and motivating employees, but caution must be used in how they are designed.

- Shareholders' agreements should clearly establish the rights, privileges and obligations of all shareholders within a company, with particular attention given to the valuation provisions, in order to avoid unintended consequences.

12 Corporate Acquisitions

We will address corporate acquisitions separately because they are often viewed as a quick way of creating shareholder value. While this can be true, corporate acquisitions can also be a quick way to erode shareholder value, if not done properly. The easiest way to buy a company is to overpay!

This chapter provides an overview of the major steps and key considerations in corporate acquisitions. If you have a keen interest in this topic, then you might enjoy another book that I wrote, entitled *The Acquisition Value Cycle*™ .[1]

The Acquisition Process

An overview of the acquisition process in what I call the *Acquisition Value Cycle*™ is illustrated below. You should be thinking about how to create shareholder value at each stage of the acquisition process.

---

1 Toronto: Carswell, 2009.

Exhibit 12A : The Acquisition Value Cycle™

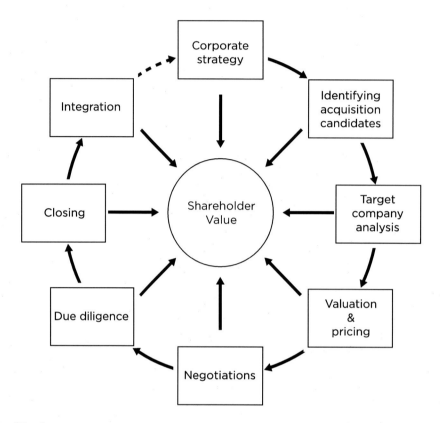

Corporate Strategy

The starting point should be a well-established corporate strategy that addresses the role acquisitions will play in helping your company to achieve its long-term objectives. In particular, your corporate strategy should address your competitive advantage and how acquisitions will serve to reinforce that competitive advantage and improve its sustainability and transferability. In the absence of a well-founded strategy, you can spend far too much time and effort chasing acquisition opportunities that simply are not a strategic fit.

You also need to know what resources you have in place, both in terms of money and people, in order to complete an acquisition. Don't underestimate the time and effort that it will take to consummate a transaction. If your management team does not have the necessary time or the expertise, it is worthwhile to engage external help.

Identifying Acquisition Targets

The next step is to identify potential acquisition targets. In this regard, you should be able to list your key acquisition criteria on one piece of paper. Criteria may include target company size, product and service offerings, customer base, geographic coverage and other parameters. Having pre-established criteria is important in order to avoid spending time and effort on opportunities that clearly are not a strategic fit.

If acquisitions are an important part of your corporate strategy, then it's not sufficient for you to just tell your lawyer, accountant and banker that you are looking for acquisitions. Rather, you should proactively search for acquisition targets by contacting the owner or senior executive of companies that may be a fit. You would be surprised how often this approach results in opportunities that you just didn't know existed. A proactive strategy can also help you to lock up acquisition opportunities before they come to market and you get caught up in a bidding war.

Target Company Analysis

Target company analysis involves performing an initial review of the information that you receive regarding an acquisition target. This usually includes some level of financial and operational data that is provided, once you have signed a non-disclosure agreement. The most important things to consider at this stage are:

    (i) whether the acquisition target represents a strategic fit, consistent with your corporate strategy; and

    (ii) the likelihood that the acquisition target can be integrated with your company's existing operations.

If you have significant doubt on either of these two aspects, then you should pass on the opportunity.

You also need to assess the *transition risk* relating to an acquisition target. Transition risk refers to the risk of losing major customers or key employees shortly after the transaction is completed. In other words, discovering after the transaction that the competitive advantage you acquired was not as sustainable or transferable as you had originally believed. Transition risk is of particular concern when you acquire a smaller company that is dependent on the involvement of its owner or a handful of individuals.

Valuation and Pricing

Based on the initial information that you receive, you should be able to conduct some preliminary valuation and pricing, using the valuation multiples approaches and discounted cash flow approach presented in Part I. As a buyer, you should think about valuation in terms of goal posts, with one end representing the value of the target company absent any synergies, and the other end representing the maximum amount you would be willing to pay, inclusive of synergies. The extent to which synergies are paid for in a transaction usually is a function of the negotiating strength of the parties involved and the structure of the transaction. These factors are discussed later in this chapter. Remember that valuation and pricing are not static. Your valuation and pricing analysis will evolve as more information becomes available throughout the acquisition process.

Pricing analysis should take into account deal structuring (which is addressed later in this chapter) and how the transaction will be financed. You also need to factor in the integration costs that will be incurred.

Remember to carefully consider what you are buying – i.e., tangible assets vs. intangible value. To the extent that you acquire intangible value, it's important to link it back to the target company's competitive advantage, and to assess the sustainability and transferability of that value.

Negotiations

Negotiations are a key aspect in any transaction. The negotiations between buyer and seller culminate in the execution of a letter of intent (LOI), which sets out the expected price and terms of the deal. While the terms of the deal as set out in the LOI are non-binding, the LOI does bind the seller from the standpoint of exclusivity granted to the buyer for an agreed period of time. Consequently, once the LOI is agreed to by the seller, the buyer enjoys a better negotiating position due to the legal and practical difficulties facing the seller in furthering their discussions with other potential suitors. By extension, a key negotiating tactic for you as a buyer is to lock up exclusivity at an early stage so as to leverage your negotiating position. The converse is true when you are a seller!

Further considerations in negotiating a deal from the buyer's perspective are discussed later in this chapter. Negotiating strategies and tactics from the sellers' perspective are discussed in Chapter 17.

Due Diligence

Due diligence involves verifying all of the facts and assumptions that you made when valuing the acquisition target and when preparing the LOI. It's a comprehensive process that usually requires external assistance from accountants, legal counsel, industry experts and others. Don't underestimate the time and effort required to conduct proper due diligence on an acquisition target.

If issues are uncovered during the due diligence investigation that were not previously known, then you will have to determine how to proceed. If the issue is not significant, then the seller may agree to accept a lower purchase price or to change the terms of the deal (e.g., more money held in escrow pending the outcome of a newly-identified potential liability). However, if the newly-identified issue causes a serious change to your assessment of transition risk or other significant risk, then it may be better to walk away.

Closing

The closing of the transaction involves the preparation of the formal purchase and sale agreement and related agreements (e.g., non-compete, management contracts, etc.). The formal closing typically takes place at a lawyer's office, where shares, cash and other considerations are exchanged, either concurrently with the signing of the purchase and sale agreement or shortly thereafter.

Integration

Buying another company is the easy part. Once the transaction is complete, the real work begins. The importance of a well-executed integration plan cannot be understated. In this regard, communication is key. Remember that employees, customers and suppliers will be anxious to know how the transaction will affect them. Therefore, frequent, clear and credible information must be provided to all stakeholders. No news is worse than bad news. Successful acquirers usually establish a *100-Day plan*, which sets out in detail all of the key things that need to happen within the first 100 days following the transaction (e.g., customer meetings, compensation adjustments, technology conversion, etc.), and who is responsible for those initiatives.

Where a private company is acquired, then following the closing, the buyer will engage its auditors to conduct an audit of the closing balance sheet, which may lead to a purchase price adjustment on account of working capital or other items. Where the target is a public company, then the buyer assumes the "balance sheet risk" after closing, which should be considered when pricing the deal.

Successful integration also requires that you assign a champion who is dedicated to the task. This cannot be a part-time role. The individual assigned must be given the authority to react quickly to deal with issues regarding employees, customers, suppliers and other integration problems. No planning is ever so complete as to foresee every possible issue that might arise, so flexibility is important.

In the end, the *Acquisition Value Cycle*™ comes full circle, with the acquired entity now forming part of your company's evolving corporate strategy.

Creating Shareholder Value Through Acquisitions

In Chapter 6, we learned how growth does not necessarily translate into higher shareholder value. This concept applies to acquisitions. While the acquisition of another company should increase the combined revenues and profitability for your company on a pro forma basis, you have not created shareholder value if the benefits of the acquisition have been fully paid for.

In the context of corporate acquisitions, shareholder value is created where one or more of the following occurs:

- the target company is acquired for less than its intrinsic value. This is a function of the relative negotiating capabilities and negotiating strategies of the buyer and seller;

- the structure of the deal reduces purchase price (in present value terms) or the risk to the buyer; or

- synergies are realized following the transaction, in excess of those which were paid for.

Negotiations

I've often referred to mergers and acquisitions (M&A) negotiations as a combination of three games:

(i) Sudoku (the Japanese number puzzle), because the numbers have to work out;

(ii) chess, for its strategic elements; and

(iii) poker, given that you are looking for "tells" from the other side.

In most situations, the seller controls the sale process and the buyer tries to react in a way that helps better their negotiating position. Effective negotiating strategies begin with information management. You should seek to understand why the seller wants (or needs) to sell. This will give you some insight into the likelihood that a transaction will occur, and the types of buyers the seller may be soliciting. It will also provide some insight into the factors that might be important to the seller beyond price (e.g., employee retention).

By the same token, it's important for you to manage the information that you provide to the seller. Remember that a trained intermediary acting on behalf of the seller will probe your acquisition team for information on strategic fit, synergy expectations and so on, in order to better understand the maximum price that your company might be willing to pay. To the extent that you divulge specific information about these things at any point in the acquisition process, it may come back to haunt you during negotiations.

Both the buyer and the seller will be driven by the number and quality of the alternatives available to them with respect to a transaction. Therefore, you should examine the marketplace for companies that have been active acquirers within your industry (both strategic buyers and financial buyers), which will help you to assess the level and type of competition you may be facing.

The buyer usually wants to gain exclusivity as early as possible in order to solidify their negotiating position. The seller usually wants to create an auction and to play one buyer off against another. So you need to understand the seller's sale process. In order to conduct an effective auction, the seller will look to receive offers at around the same time. You can gain some insight into the seller's sale process and the quality of their alternatives by changing the pace of discussions in an effort to disrupt the pure auction. For example, if the seller tells you that you must submit your offer by a certain date, a good tactic is to try extending that date. If the seller's reaction is to allow consecutive extensions, it suggests that they have not yet received a satisfactory offer from another party.

Being flexible in terms of the structure of the deal can also give you a negotiating advantage. Many sellers focus on the price they are getting for their company, and they do not pay adequate attention to the terms of the deal. Deal structuring is discussed in the next section.

Finally, it's important to establish a limit as to the price you are willing to pay and to stick with it. Remember that acquisitions should be viewed as one means of achieving your strategic objectives, and that other alternatives exist (e.g., build vs. buy or joint ventures). Before you submit an offer, be sure to ask yourself, "What am I buying?" and "To what extent does the purchase price represent tangible net worth vs. intangible value?" In most cases, you can readily replace a company's tangible net worth, so you are really paying a premium for the intangible aspects of the acquisition target. You have to ensure that the target company's competitive advantage that gives rise to its intangible value is both sustaining and transferable, or you will have overpaid.

Deal Structuring

The terms of the deal are just as important as the stated purchase price. There are three main parameters to deal structuring, which are:

• whether the assets or the shares of the target company are acquired;

• the forms of consideration (including terms of payment); and

• management contracts with the seller.

Buyers usually prefer to buy the assets of a target company because it can give rise to tax advantages, and it helps in avoiding hidden liabilities. Furthermore, asset deals sometimes are less complicated from the standpoint of indemnities, holdbacks and other protection mechanisms sought by the buyer. However, sellers typically prefer to sell shares in order to benefit from lower taxes on capital gains. Therefore, a buyer may be willing to pay a higher price for assets than for shares. A purchase of shares may also facilitate the transaction where contracts and agreements would not have to be assigned as they would in an asset deal. Share deals are also more common in the takeover of a public company.

The forms of consideration address how, when and the conditions under which the purchase price is (or is not) paid. Where the acquisition target is a public company, the buyer usually has minimal flexibility with respect to forms of consideration. This is because the entire purchase price has to be paid on closing, either in the form of cash or shares of the buyer. However, the acquisition of a private company (or a division of a public company) can give rise to considerable flexibility in terms of deal structuring. Apart from cash on closing, common forms of consideration include holdbacks, promissory notes, share exchanges and earnouts.

Buyers use holdbacks to offset the risk of acquiring assets that cannot be realized (e.g., uncollectible accounts receivable) or hidden liabilities after the closing date. Holdbacks normally represent between 10% and 20% of the purchase price, and are released over a period of six months to two years.

Promissory notes are used where the buyer does not have sufficient funds to finance the deal on closing. Promissory notes may or may not be interest-bearing and normally are repaid over the course of one to five years. The payment of promissory notes sometimes is linked to indemnifications provided by the seller.

Share exchanges occur where the seller agrees to exchange shares of their company for shares in the buyer's company. This form of consideration is most commonly used by small-cap and mid-cap public companies that use their own shares as currency in lieu of cash. Share exchanges can be attractive because, where properly structured, they offer the seller a tax deferral for the amount of the sale proceeds. However, sellers often resist share exchanges given the risk that the shares they acquire may decline in value or may not be readily saleable, particularly where there are legal or practical restrictions imposed on liquidating those shares in the public markets.

Earnout arrangements occur where the buyer agrees to pay the seller a higher price in the event that certain performance targets are met following the transaction. Performance targets can be based on sales, profitability or other measures, and normally last for a period of one to five years. In effect, an earnout represents a transfer of risk from the buyer to the seller. Therefore, earnouts represent an effective risk mitigation strategy for the buyer.

Another way to mitigate risk is to buy more than 50%, but less than 100%, of the target company. This will give you control, but will also ensure the continued efforts of the seller in building shareholder value since they retain a residual interest. It also reduces the amount of your initial cash outlay. The shareholders' agreement should contain provisions regarding the terms and conditions that govern the subsequent acquisition of the residual interest.

The provisions of a management or consulting contract can be quite varied in terms of duration and scope. It defines the role and responsibilities of the seller under the new ownership, as well as the basis of remuneration. The duration of a management contract normally ranges from six months to five years. An effective tactic is to offer the seller a lucrative compensation package in lieu of a higher price for their company. This gives the buyer a tax advantage (at the expense of the seller) since salary payments are tax deductible, and it instills a greater level of "pay for performance". As a practical matter, longer-term management contracts often are never fulfilled in their entirety due to issues that arise regarding performance, expectations or differences in culture, to which the seller finds it difficult to adapt. Therefore, you should ensure that a succession plan is in place in order to mitigate transition risk.

So the message here is that it's not just what you pay, it's the value of what you get in return that's important. When dealing with the acquisition of a private company, there is often a way to meet the seller's price expectations without giving up as much in "value". Where some of the purchase price is paid over time, or is structured as a tax-deductible payment to the buyer, then the after-tax present value of the purchase price is lower, thereby helping to create shareholder value.

As a buyer, you should focus on implementing a *value-based pricing strategy,* which entails trying to match the benefits of the acquisition with the payment of the purchase price, though holdbacks, earnouts, management contracts and other pay-for-performance incentives. This helps in reducing risk and, by extension, increasing shareholder value. The ability to implement a value-based pricing strategy will depend on your relative negotiating position, given the seller's need to transact and their alternatives in that regard.

Synergies

A key consideration in most acquisitions is how much the buyer expects to realize in terms of post-acquisition synergies. Synergies are unique to every buyer. Common sources of synergies include the following:

- increased revenues from the combined entity due to cross-selling opportunities;

- cost savings due to consolidation of facilities, headcount reductions or other initiatives; and

- risk reduction of the combined entity, such as where the target company has access to a critical input that the buyer needs in its operations.

Buyers typically do not want to pay for all of the synergies they anticipate. First, because most buyers perceive that the synergies are "theirs" and, secondly, because the buyer perceives risk in realizing some or all the synergy component. Ultimately, whether and to what extent, those synergies are paid for is a function of the negotiations and deal structuring.

It's easy to get carried away with synergy expectations. However, you should recognize that there is a cost associated with realizing synergies (e.g., severance costs associated with headcount reductions). Furthermore, many synergies do not materialize to the extent anticipated. Where synergies are fully paid for, there is no buffer to allow for shortfalls.

In the context of a potential transaction, it's helpful to assess synergies as a separate component of value. As a general rule, you should figure on 50% of expected synergies not being realized and that it will take twice as long as anticipated in order to realize those synergies that do materialize.

Let's return to our example of Tasty Snacks Ltd., which is considering the acquisition of Yummy Treats Inc. Yummy Treats generates $5 million in EBITDA on revenues of $50 million. In assessing the potential value of synergies, Tasty Snacks has assumed the following:

- Headcount reductions could be achieved for savings of $500,000 per annum (growing at inflation). Severance costs would be $250,000;

- Some cross-selling opportunities exist, which will allow Tasty Snacks to generate incremental revenues of $1 million in the first year, $2 million in the second year, $3 million in the third year, and growing at 3% per year thereafter. The incremental profit margin is estimated at 20%; and

- In order to effectively integrate the operations of Yummy Treats, Tasty Snacks will incur $500,000 of up-front expenses.

Exhibit 12B : Tasty Snacks Ltd. Estimated Synergies from Yummy Treats Acquisition $(000)

		Forecast			
		Year 1	Year 2	Year 3	Thereafter
Revenues		1,000	2,000	3,000	3,090
% Growth					3%
Incremental profit margin at	20%	200	400	600	618
Headcount savings		500	510	520	531
Pretax benefit		700	910	1,120	1,149
Income taxes at	30%	(210)	(270)	(340)	(345)
Incremental discretionary cash flow		490	640	780	804
Capitalization rate					10%
Terminal value					8,040
Discounted cash flow					
# of years forward (mid-point)		0.5	1.5	2.5	2.5
Discount factor at	13%	0.941	0.832	0.737	0.737
		460	530	570	5,900

Increase in enterprise value (rounded)	7,500	
Probability factor	50%	
Probabilized net economic benefit	3,750	
Initial costs		
Severance	(250)	
Integration costs	(500)	
Total	(750)	
Less: tax savings thereon	30%	230
Net costs	(520)	
Net economic benefit	**3,230**	

Note how in this analysis the expected benefits were assigned a probability factor of 50%, but that no probability factor was applied to the initial costs. While this might be a somewhat conservative approach, it serves to highlight the reality that costs are usually more certain than benefits.

Common Mistakes in Acquisitions

Research has shown that most corporate acquisitions fail to achieve their desired results. Some acquisitions are downright disastrous. The most common reason for deal failure is poor integration. Buyers often leave integration as an afterthought rather than addressing potential integration issues up front and establishing a sound integration plan at an early stage. Poor integration usually results in lost customers or key employees, which is the essence of intangible value in many companies.

Overpaying for synergies is another common issue. Buyers frequently overestimate the potential rewards from an acquisition and do not give adequate consideration to the costs of achieving synergies, the time that it takes for synergies to be realized or the risk attaching to synergy realization. They also forget to fully consider integration costs.

Inadequate due diligence also surfaces as a root cause of deal failure. The result is hidden costs and unidentified issues that must be dealt with post-closing. Buyers of privately-held companies sometimes make the mistake of relying on the seller's representations and warranties in the purchase and sale agreement in order to compensate for inadequate due diligence. However, it's important to recognize that thorough due diligence is critical in order to identify those areas where representations and warranties are needed.

Many buyers make technical errors in their financial analysis and valuation models. This is even true among large companies with dedicated M&A departments. The models for discounted cash flow can become quite large and complex, and it's easy for errors in spreadsheets to go undetected. That's why it's helpful to support any discounted cash flow analysis with reasonableness tests such as implied valuation multiples.

In other cases, buyers rely too much on multiples of EBITDA as a basis for valuation and pricing. Recall from Chapter 2 that EBITDA does not specifically address key components of shareholder value such as capital spending requirements, working capital and taxation. These factors are specifically addressed in the DCF methodology.

Most deals are consummated following hard negotiations between the buyer and seller. Sometimes things get said or inferred during those negotiations that leaves a bitter sentiment for the seller after closing. This makes the integration efforts more difficult and leads to increased transition risk. In order to prevent this from happening, buyers are wise to engage an intermediary to conduct negotiations on their behalf, so that they can be somewhat removed from any bitter sentiment.

Finally, many buyers do not exercise self-discipline. They fall in love with the prospect of doing a deal, especially where they have spent a lot of time and effort trying to make it happen. This causes the buyer to gravitate away from the economic fundamentals and let themselves believe that a premium price can be justified through some hidden source of value. Unfortunately, this seldom is the case.

Exhibit 12C : Common Mistakes in Acquisitions

- Poor integration

- Overpaying for synergies

- Inadequate due diligence

- Technical errors in financial analysis

- Over-reliance on multiples of EBITDA

- Bitter post-acquisition sentiment

- Falling in love with the deal

Key Points to Remember

- Creating shareholder value through acquisitions rests in your negotiating capabilities, as well as the structure of the deal and synergy realization.

- Effective negotiations start with information management, including an understanding of what's important from the seller's perspective and the alternatives that the seller has available.

- Try to employ a risk-based pricing strategy, so that the payment of the purchase price is tied to future performance, at least to some degree.

- Synergies should be critically assessed to determine the risk and cost associated with their realization.

- The most common mistakes made by corporate acquirers include poorly executed integration, overpaying for synergies and inadequate due diligence.

PART III VALUE REALIZATION

13 Avenues to Value Realization

A t some point, business owners and executives will want to ensure that the value that has been created within their company is realized. There are several ways that value realization can be accomplished, ranging from liquidating your company all the way through to an initial public offering. Each possible avenue has various trade-offs that must be carefully considered in order for you to make an informed decision.

Value realization is a function of liquidity and alternatives. In order for you to make an informed decision, it's important to understand all of the viable alternatives for value realization that are available, and the pros and cons of each, even if some avenues may not appear particularly attractive.

"Value realization" is the ability to convert shareholder value into cash. Where shareholder value is converted to some other form of consideration (e.g., a promissory note on the sale of your company), an element of risk still remains. This is an important principle to remember: *any dollar not received at the closing of a transaction represents a dollar at risk.* You have to be satisfied that the prospective reward is worth the risk.

This chapter provides an overview of some of the avenues available for value realization. Subsequent chapters will delve more deeply into the topics of family business succession, financial buyers, management buyouts and strategic buyers.

A Spectrum of Alternatives

The alternatives for realizing shareholder value can be categorized in one of three ways:

1. shareholder distributions, whereby the shareholders withdraw their capital out of a company by way of liquidation, dividends/share buybacks or recapitalization;

2. related party transactions, i.e., a transaction involving parties that are already involved with a company. This includes a sale to other existing shareholders, family succession and management buyouts; and

3. transactions with third parties, i.e., a transaction involving parties that are outside of a company. This includes financial buyers, strategic buyers and initial public offerings.

As illustrated in Exhibit 13A, as you proceed along this spectrum of alternatives, the potential for reward increases, but so does your exposure to risk. In addition, many of these alternatives overlap. For example, a management buyout often is combined with a debt recapitalization and/or the support of a financial buyer.

Exhibit 13A : Avenues to Value Realization

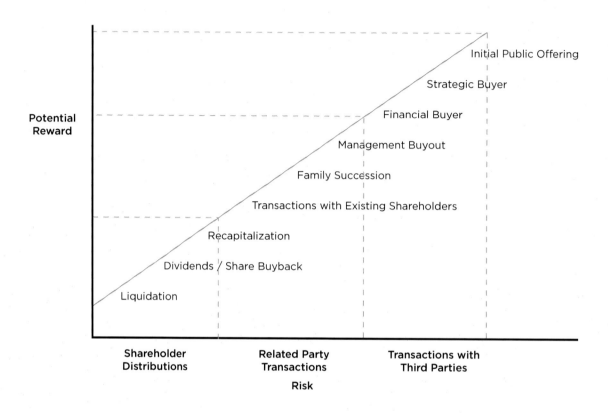

Shareholder Distributions

Liquidation

Liquidation is seldom the best way to maximize shareholder value. However, it sometimes represents a plausible alternative, especially if a buyer or successor for your company cannot be found. Furthermore, in some cases, the net proceeds that would be realized upon liquidation may be greater than the amount a buyer would pay to acquire your company. This might occur if your company has incurred several years of losses or where economic conditions are such that few buyers are coming to the table.

When you are considering any value realization event for your company, it's helpful to estimate the net proceeds that would be realized upon liquidation, even if that option is not being contemplated, because it represents the worst case scenario. In any negotiating situation, you need to understand your alternatives, even if they are not particularly attractive.

There are two basic liquidation scenarios, referred to as a *forced liquidation* and a *voluntary liquidation*. A forced liquidation occurs where a company's creditors force it into bankruptcy because they are not being paid. In most cases involving a forced liquidation, the secured creditors are able to recover some of their debts, whereas unsecured creditors often receive little or nothing. By extension, there is rarely any residual value that remains for the shareholders.

In the case of a voluntary liquidation, the shareholders generally expect to realize some value for their equity interest. In most cases involving a voluntary liquidation, the operations of the company are wound down slowly, with the objective of collecting outstanding accounts receivable and selling off remaining inventories. Fixed assets are usually sold at auction for their salvage value. Where intangible assets exist that have some legal substance to them (e.g., patents), these can sometimes be converted to cash as well.

However, in most cases involving a voluntary liquidation, the shareholders should expect that they will not fully recover the retained earnings in their company because of the costs of winding up the operations in an orderly fashion. This usually entails offering remaining employees some incentive package and/or severance payments to remain with the company through the wind-up period. Furthermore, there can be costs associated with unsaleable inventories, lease cancellations, etc., and the value received for fixed assets typically is less than their net book value. Consequently, even in a voluntary liquidation, there may be little or no residual value to the shareholders once all of the costs associated with discontinuing operations have been settled.

Dividends/Share Buybacks

The simplest way to realize shareholder value from your company is to pay yourself a dividend (or remuneration in excess of market rates), or alternatively to redeem some of the outstanding shares. Special dividends and share buybacks are common among publicly held companies that find themselves with more cash than they need. In the case of a privately-held company, the choice between dividends, excess remuneration and share buybacks typically is driven by tax efficiency.

Dividends and share buybacks are an efficient and relatively low-risk way to withdraw excess cash from your company. However, it's only a partial solution, since the non-cash component of shareholder value remains intact.

If dividend distributions are to be a mechanism for ongoing shareholder value realization, then you need to ensure the sustainability of your company's competitive advantage. This becomes somewhat of a "Catch-22" situation, since the more cash you drain from your company, the less able it is to reinvest in the initiatives that sustain value. This includes ensuring that the right management team is in place in order to generate an adequate return on invested capital over the long term.

Recapitalization

In many cases, the existing shareholders are not ready to sell their company or to pass it along to the next generation. However, they would like to "take some chips off the table". This can be accomplished by injecting debt into your company and declaring a large one-time dividend or share redemption. Similarly, in the case of a public company, where the operations are relatively stable and cash will not be required for growth, it can make sense to replace equity with debt.

Where the recapitalization only involves senior debt, the existing shareholders are able to maintain full control of the company at a relatively low cost. Subordinated debt and mezzanine financing may also be available, but the cost is higher, and it may involve an element of equity participation.

In Chapter 10 the "magic of financial leverage" was illustrated, i.e., the return on the tangible net worth can be magnified by replacing equity with debt. However, this comes at the expense of greater *financial risk*, which has to be taken into account. Therefore, a *recapitalization does not create shareholder value*, rather it provides higher *possible* shareholder returns in exchange for higher risk. Whether or not those returns are realized will only be known after the fact.

Consider our ongoing example of Tasty Snacks Ltd., which needs to finance net operating assets of $40 million. In Chapter 10 we discussed the trade-off between the amount of senior debt financing and the return on tangible net worth, which can be illustrated as follows:

Exhibit 13B : Tasty Snacks Ltd. Return on Tangible Net Worth

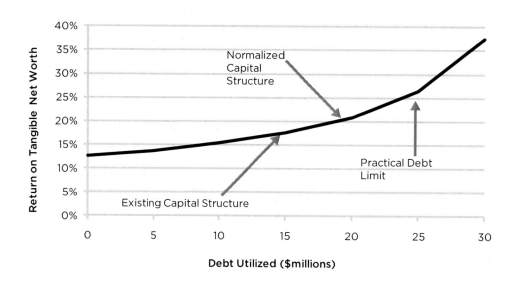

While the potential returns at the far end of the chart may appear attractive (a 37% return on tangible net worth based on using $30 million of debt), they are impractical. Given its cash flows and the underlying assets that could be used as security, Tasty Snacks would not be able to raise such high levels of senior debt financing to achieve these types of returns. As was illustrated in Chapter 4, management of Tasty Snacks believes that a normalized amount of senior debt is about $20 million.

Also recall that more debt within your company leads to more restrictive covenants that have to be observed, which may reduce your ability to undertake capital investments that help build shareholder value, or to declare dividends in order to realize shareholder value. These restrictions can become particularly acute where your company experiences an economic downturn, and cash flow becomes constrained.

The flip side is that a recapitalization allows the shareholders to acquire investments outside of your company. Many business owners have most of their personal wealth invested in their company, which can be devastating in the event that the company fails due to changing market conditions or some other unforeseen event. By removing capital from your company and investing the proceeds into a portfolio of stocks and bonds, your shareholders can achieve better diversification.

Related Party Transactions

Transactions Among Existing Shareholders

In companies having more than one shareholder, a common avenue for liquidity is transactions among existing shareholders. Such transactions can arise as a result of the desire by a shareholder to leave the company (e.g., retirement of an individual or a change in strategy for a corporate shareholder), the death of a shareholder, a shareholder dispute or a variety of other reasons.

As noted in Chapter 11, transactions among shareholders should be governed by a well-documented shareholders' agreement, failing which there could be significant disagreement as to the price and terms of sale. The specific provisions governing valuation (including the possible application of a minority discount) and terms of payment are particularly relevant.

In many cases, the share price for transactions among existing shareholders is established pursuant to an independent valuation. In this regard, it's helpful if all shareholders agree to jointly retain an independent valuation firm and agree to be bound by the value conclusions. This helps to avoid extensive time and cost where multiple valuation firms are engaged and the differences in conclusions must be reconciled or arbitrated.

In the case of a public company, it's common to get a fairness opinion for transactions involving related parties, for the purpose of satisfying securities commissions' requirements and as a matter of good governance. In this regard, the fairness opinion should be rendered by a firm that is viewed as independent, in both fact and appearance.

Family Succession

For many business owners, their dream is to transfer their company to the next generation. In such cases, the existing shareholders typically realize value either pursuant to a buyout by family members over time, or by taking back preferred shares that are redeemed upon death or at some other date. Therefore, the realization of shareholder value is deferred (and subject to risk). The structure of the transaction is driven more by the objective of ensuring a smooth succession than immediate value realization.

Despite good intentions, family business succession can be fraught with challenges, particularly where there are multiple family members with divergent needs and interests. Consequently, relatively few family businesses survive beyond the third generation. Some of the challenges and possible solutions to family succession are covered in the next chapter.

Management Buyouts

Management buyouts refer to situations where a company's management team acquires the equity interests of the existing shareholders. The advantage of a management buyout is that it tends to be quicker and more confidential than selling to a strategic buyer, since management is already familiar with the company.

The challenge is that management rarely has sufficient capital to effect the transaction on their own. Therefore, management buyouts usually entail some third party financing, in the form of senior debt, mezzanine financing, private equity financing or a combination thereof. Even where this is the case, the existing shareholders often find themselves having to take some of the payment over time, thereby exposing them to ongoing risk. Management buyouts are discussed in detail in Chapter 16.

Transactions with Third Parties

Financial Buyers

Selling to a "financial buyer" is the sale of your company to a private equity firm or to a buyer that views your company as a portfolio investment rather than as a long-term acquisition that will be integrated with its existing operations. Financial buyers are looking to earn a return on their investment through ongoing cash flow from your company and the eventual resale of your company at a profit. In many cases, financial buyers will use significant amounts of debt to effect the transaction. Where only a small amount of equity is used, the transaction is often referred to as a *leveraged buyout*.

In many cases, financial buyers look to engage the existing management team with an equity commitment or as part of a management buyout. The possible returns to the individual management team members who participate can be quite lucrative, as illustrated in Chapter 16.

Selling to a financial buyer often is viewed as an interim step for existing shareholders in a company. Recall that some private equity firms will take on a minority ownership position as a means of allowing existing shareholders to "take chips off the table". However, the provisions of the shareholders' agreement usually provides the financial buyer with considerable protection.

In other cases, the existing shareholders may want to sell a controlling interest to a private equity firm but retain a meaningful residual interest in order to enjoy some potential for gain. Many private equity firms prefer that existing shareholders who are actively involved in the company retain a residual ownership interest in order to ensure their continued commitment and to help facilitate a smooth transition. The dynamics of selling to a financial buyer are discussed in Chapter 15.

Strategic Buyers

Strategic buyers are often viewed as the best avenue for maximizing shareholder value. This is true in many cases, particularly where a strategic buyer views your company as a *platform* investment that it can leverage to generate significant synergies *and* where the strategic buyer has sufficient financial resources available to effect the transaction on attractive terms.

However, selling to a strategic buyer can also be fraught with challenges, ranging from maintaining confidentiality to deal structuring. The key to realizing shareholder value with a strategic buyer is to ensure that you control the sale process and leverage your negotiating position. Selling to strategic buyers is discussed in Chapter 17.

Initial Public Offerings (IPOs)

Many business owners and executives consider an initial public offering as a means of realizing shareholder value. The valuation multiples inferred by the public equity markets are often greater than those which are offered by financial or strategic buyers. However, initial public offerings are more often associated with financing growth as the primary objective, whereby the existing shareholders may only receive a portion of the proceeds raised. This is particularly the case for smaller companies, where the public markets are skeptical if existing shareholders are looking to "cash out". That said, an IPO affords shareholders with a mechanism for ongoing liquidity, subject to certain trading restrictions.

There are numerous advantages and disadvantages to going public that should be carefully considered, which were addressed in Chapter 11.

Key Points to Remember

- Create several alternatives for liquidity, and ensure that you understand the pros and cons of each.

- Any dollar not received at the closing of a transaction represents a dollar at risk, and you must be satisfied that the potential reward is worth the risk.

- Beware that when using dividends and share buybacks as a means of realizing shareholder value that you do not withdraw so much cash as to jeopardize the ability of your company to sustain its competitive advantage.

- While the use of debt to recapitalize your company can serve to magnify shareholder returns, it does not, in itself, create shareholder value.

- While an initial public offering can create liquidity for shareholders, it is more often used in conjunction with growth financing, which is more appealing to public equity market investors.

14 Family Business Succession

If you own or manage a family business, then you know first-hand the unique challenges that are involved. Decisions surrounding family business succession planning tend to be difficult and complex because both family personalities and the family business are closely related. As a practical matter, relatively few family businesses last more than three generations because of the complexities and dynamics involved in passing wealth through generations, where each generation involves a larger number of stakeholders.

In this chapter, I'll discuss some of the challenges relating to family business succession and possible solutions to help in that regard.

Planning for the Transition

Families are comprised of individuals with a wide range of abilities, ambitions, motivations, emotional stability, social values and level of interest in the family business from an operations point of view. Consequently, family members can bring emotional and intellectual baggage to a family business that does not exist to the same degree in non-family businesses. As a result of these and other things, irrespective of interests and good intentions, family business succession planning generally is a process of deferral and procrastination.

As a first step, family members should seek to objectively determine whether the family business is going to be viable over the medium to longer term in the face of changing industry and economic conditions. This is paramount to determining what should be done with the family business (i.e., operate vs. sell). Too often, families decide to continue operating the business for the sake of "preserving its legacy" rather than basing their decision on sound economic principles, which can lead to unfortunate results. Assessing long-term business viability and options should be a formal annual process and should involve the input of objective and competent advisors.

Forecasting financial results is fundamental to family succession or sale decision making, where forecasting encompasses likely fundamental changes, both near-term and long-term, to the micro and macro business conditions of the company. Without a carefully documented long-term strategic plan, decisions regarding family succession or sale cannot be made on an informed basis. A family succession plan likely will fail without such a strategic plan being fully documented.

Family succession planning has the greatest chance of success if the founder or builders decide its course at a time when there are a workable number of family member shareholders. As the number of family participants increases with each passing generation, the succession issue becomes exponentially more complex. This is not to suggest that any family member shareholders should be denied input into the family succession process. Rather, if there are competent authority figures involved in the family business at the time family succession planning is agreed and implemented, there is a much greater likelihood of such agreement and implementation.

Components of Effective Family Business Succession

Family members have divergent needs and interests. In particular, as a family business evolves there tend to be two distinct groups of family shareholders: (i) those actively involved in the family business; and (ii) those that are not actively involved. These two factions often disagree with respect to the strategic direction and governance of the family business.

As a matter of practice, in order for family business succession to succeed, the following need to be in place:

- a strategized evolution of a family corporation from an entrepreneurial base to a professionally managed business. Family business owners contemplating the viability of family ownership succession must be able to clearly separate their business goals from their personal goals;

- common family shareholder risk profiles. This ensures that family members are consistent in their thinking with respect to the overall strategic direction of the company, the magnitude of debt financing and other decisions that significantly impact the risk profile of the family business;

- common agreement among family shareholders with respect to the importance of, and the implementation of, meaningful corporate governance involving (among other things) a Board of Directors having a representation of non-family members;

- a clear distinction of who will own and who will manage the company. In this regard, there must be a high level of confidence in family management by all family shareholders. Family members active in the management of the company must be viewed as having earned those positions, both by other family members and non-family members. It's often advisable for family members to work outside of the family business for a number of years and to then actively choose to join the family business; and

- remuneration of family members active in the management of the company that approximates an arm's length equivalency, and is perceived as such by family members not active in the management of the business. As with any privately-held company, there should be a distinction between *return on labour* and *return on capital*. A compensation committee comprised of independent (non-family) directors can be helpful in this regard.

Finally, shareholders' agreements are a key element for any family business. Unfortunately, they are often not executed because they are considered taboo in a family business context. However, a properly structured shareholders' agreement that establishes the rights, privileges and obligations of all shareholders within the family business is an important step in helping all family members to recognize that their equity interest in the family business should be viewed from an economic perspective and not just from the standpoint of personal sentiment.

Exhibit 14A : Components of Effective Family Business Succession

- Evolution from entrepreneurial to professional corporation
- Common risk profiles
- Common corporate governance expectations
- Distinction between ownership and management
- Market-based compensation for family managers

Effecting the Family Business Succession Plan

Fundamental to effecting the family business succession plan is the determination of whether it is to be structured as a tax-deferred transfer or an actual sale to family members. The family business owners also have to determine whether the transaction involves only their children, or other family members, such as siblings, cousins or other relationships. The more removed the family members, the greater the succession process reflects an arm's length sale.

Exhibit 14B : Family Business Succession Parameters

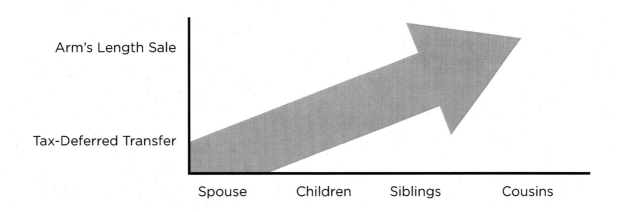

Tax-deferred intergenerational transfers tend to be relatively simple to effect. In essence, the business owner undertakes an estate freeze, whereby they establish the value of the company at a point in time and exchange their existing common shares for preferred shares for that stated amount. The preferred shares have a redemption value equal to the freeze value, and normally are redeemed on death. As such, it is advisable for the company to secure adequate life insurance on the business owner effecting the freeze so that sufficient capital is available to redeem the shares on death, and pay the resultant taxes at that time.

Upon the freeze, the company issues new common shares to the next generation of family members, which initially have minimal value. Increasing the value of the newly issued common shares rests in the ability for the company to generate incremental value over the freeze amount. In most cases, business owners undertaking an estate freeze have a "low value bias" in order to afford the greatest potential for gain for the next generation of owners. However, the tax authorities will usually require an independent valuation from qualified experts in order to justify the freeze amount, failing which there could be penalties or other consequences.

Where cash proceeds or some other form of consideration actually changes hands in a family business succession event, several issues can arise. The first issue is financing. The personal relationship among family members will often dictate the degree to which the seller offers financing to the buyer in the form of a promissory note, earnout arrangement or other deferred payment structure. Where third party financing is secured, the financing structure usually is in the form of senior debt. Private equity firms generally will not invest in a family succession scenario given the likely absence of a liquidity event in the near term.

Another issue is taxation. Transactions among individuals that do not act at arm's length must be conducted at fair market value. Failure to do so can have adverse consequences to both the buyer and seller. Therefore, as a business owner you are well advised to retain competent tax advice as well as an independent valuation, where required, in order to circumvent these issues.

Family Business Succession Challenges

It's unusual for families owning businesses to successfully implement and achieve multi-generational family business transfers (i.e., pass operating businesses and pooled family wealth into successive generations) unless there is significant wealth within the family unit. This is because the absolute number of family members usually expands in succeeding generations more quickly than the pooled family wealth. Consequently, relatively few family businesses survive beyond the third generation of family business owners.

As the pool of family member owners expands, many challenges can arise, including:

- greater differences in individual risk profiles and liquidity needs among family member shareholders. This makes it difficult for family members to agree on corporate strategy, governance and the degree to which the family business should be financed by debt;

- more family member shareholders who are not actively involved in the company. Absent good corporate governance, these individuals often believe that family member managers are not performing adequately or that their remuneration is excessive; and

- greater difficulty in attracting and retaining strong third party management, because they perceive limited upward career mobility in a company with numerous family members.

An effective way of reducing the challenges of having numerous non-active family members in a company is to offer all family shareholders the opportunity to liquidate their interest at a value determined pursuant to an annual valuation. In many cases, the determined value is subject to a minority discount, in order to reflect the non-controlling position of the individual interest. In addition, it is common for the seller to receive payment for their shares over some period of time, thereby reducing the need for the company to seek third party financing. The minority discount and payment terms can act as a deterrent for family shareholders who simply wish to "cash out" when the valuation of the company is favourable.

The annual valuation and minority discount must be perceived as being determined on a basis that is fair and internally consistent. By using this mechanism, family members are effectively choosing to remain as shareholders within the company. This mechanism requires that the family business have adequate liquidity in terms of cash or other liquid assets in the event that shares need to be redeemed pursuant to the "put option" afforded to family shareholders.

Key Points to Remember

- Conduct an annual assessment of the near-term and long-term viability of the family business and the relating options.

- Ensure that you segregate *return on labour* for family management, based on market rates for their individual skills and contributions to the company, and *return on capital*, where all shareholders should be treated equally.

- Implement a governance structure that promotes transparency and accountability.

- Ensure that family shareholders sign off on a well-documented shareholders' agreement.

- Create a mechanism to afford liquidity for family members desiring an exit, but based on a price and terms that will not be overly burdensome to the company.

15 Selling to Financial Buyers

A financial buyer refers to a private equity firm or other organization that views your company as a possible equity portfolio investment. While financial buyers can have very divergent investment horizons, they typically seek to profit by reselling their investments at some point in the future. For the sake of expediency, we'll refer to financial buyers as "private equity firms".

In Chapter 11, we discussed how private equity firms can be used as a source of equity financing to support your company's growth initiatives. In this chapter, the focus is on private equity firms as a possible buyer for most or all of the shares of your company (i.e., an exit strategy for existing shareholders). The use of a private equity "sponsor" in support of a management buyout is addressed in the next chapter.

What Do Private Equity Firms Look For?

There are three financial levers that private equity firms use to generate a return on their invested capital. They are:

- increasing the revenues and cash flows of the portfolio company, either through organic growth or acquisition;

- financial leverage – i.e., using debt to magnify their equity returns. It's not uncommon for private equity firms to deploy more debt in a company than would normally be used; and

- exit multiple expansion, meaning that the valuation multiple is higher when the private equity firm exits the investment (through a subsequent sale or public offering) than the valuation multiple that was paid when the investment was made.

It follows that private equity firms typically seek buyout opportunities that meet their stated investment criteria in terms of investment size, industry, life cycle stage and geographic area (see Chapter 11) and which exhibit the following characteristics:

- strong business fundamentals. Private equity firms generally are more interested in companies having a sustainable competitive advantage in the marketplace. Companies that are leaders within a market niche may be particularly attractive. Private equity firms will emphasize a company's ability to generate cash flow, both to reinvest for growth and to service debt;

- excellent growth potential, either organically or through acquisition. This feature is consistent with the private equity firm's intention on exiting the investment at some point in the future;

- a strong management team. Private equity firms generally manage their investments through a presence on a company's Board of Directors. They rely on management for both strategic input and daily operations. Therefore, private equity firms seek out dedicated management teams with a proven track record. They look for companies with strong breadth and depth in their management ranks;

- management commitment. Many private equity firms prefer that key managers personally invest in the company in order to secure their commitment. In most cases, the absolute amount of the investment is not an issue, so long as it represents a meaningful commitment by the individual(s). Managers that do invest can realize lucrative potential gain when things turn out as planned;

- alignment of interests. Private equity firms are interested in backing a company where the management team (and the existing shareholders who retain a residual interest) are intent on growing the business over the next several years and then selling it within the desired investment horizon;

- ability to leverage. Private equity firms that invest in more established or mature companies generally seek to use some amount of debt financing in order to reduce the size of their equity investment and magnify their returns. These private equity firms seek companies with quality assets and strong cash flows, which can support debt financing at reasonable rates. However, as noted in Chapter 10, it's important to recognize that higher amounts of debt financing increases financial risk, and may result in cumbersome operating restrictions. The use of debt financing is less common for early stage and venture capital-type investments; and

- exit strategy opportunities. Private equity firms generally have a three to seven-year time frame to liquidate their investment (although some firms have a longer investment horizon). They look for companies that can either be sold to a strategic buyer or are believed to be good candidates for an initial public offering within that time frame.

Exhibit 15A : Private Equity Buyout Criteria

- Business fundamentals/competitive advantage
- Growth potential
- Management team
- Management commitment
- Alignment of interests
- Ability to leverage
- Exit strategy

While threshold rates of return sought by private equity firms will vary depending on the nature of the investment, a range of 25% to 30% return on equity is not uncommon for established businesses having a defendable market position. These returns represent *levered* rates of return on equity, after debt servicing costs have been covered. Higher rates of return (often in the range of 40% to 50%) generally are sought for riskier *venture capital*-type investments.

How Do Private Equity Buyouts Work?

In our example of Tasty Snacks Ltd., let's assume that a private equity firm is looking to acquire the company for $50 million (representing 5x current EBITDA of $10 million). The financing of the deal would be comprised of $25 million in senior debt financing and $25 million in equity financing, representing a debt to equity ratio of 1:1. Recall that $25 million of debt financing is management's estimate of the company's senior debt capacity, and is higher than the estimated "normalized" debt level of $20 million. Since Tasty Snacks currently has $15 million of debt outstanding, the private equity firm would raise an additional $10 million of senior debt. Tasty Snacks expects to grow its revenues and EBIT by 10% per year.

Over the course of the next three years, the private equity firm would use any excess cash flow to reduce outstanding debt (commonly referred to as a *cash sweep*). The amount of debt outstanding is expected to increase in Year 1 to support the company's capital spending initiatives. Tasty Snacks is cash flow positive in Years 2 and 3, which can be used to repay debt. Consequently, by the end of the third year, the debt outstanding will be reduced to approximately $21.5 million. At that time, the private equity firm expects that it can sell Tasty Snacks for close to $80 million, representing a multiple of 6x Year 3 EBITDA of $13.3 million. In effect, the private equity firm believes that it can fetch a higher multiple at some point in the future if it can help Tasty Snacks to grow and to become a more attractive target to a strategic buyer. Consequently, through a combination of financial leverage, organic growth and exit multiple expansion, the private equity firm believes that it can turn its $25 million investment into more than $58 million over the next three years, thereby achieving a return on equity of 33%.

Exhibit 15B : Private Equity Buyout of Tasty Snacks $(000)

	Current Year	Forecast		
		Year 1	Year 2	Year 3
EBITDA	10,000	11,000	12,100	13,300
Multiple	5x			6x
Enterprise Value	50,000			79,800
Capital Structure				
Opening debt balance	15,000	25,000	27,860	25,121
Debt additions (repayments)	10,000	2,860	(2,739)	(3,652)
Total debt	25,000	27,860	25,121	21,469
Equity	25,000			58,331
Return on Equity				33%

Private Equity Buyers vs. Strategic Buyers

In many cases, financial buyers are viewed as "bargain hunters", and therefore a less attractive alternative to strategic buyers. However, this is not always the case. Where a private equity firm has an existing portfolio investment in a specific industry sector and they are looking at a company as a "bolt-on" opportunity, the private equity firm may be prepared to pay a *strategic value*. Furthermore, many private equity firms have more capital available than strategic buyers, so that the cash component of the deal could be more attractive to the seller.

When selling your company, it's important to understand the mentality and the objectives of the buyer. Strategic buyers and private equity firms can be quite different in this regard. While each buyer is unique, a general comparison of the key differences between strategic buyers and private equity firms is as follows:

• strategic buyers undertake acquisitions from the standpoint of a long-term investment horizon, whereas private equity firms are focused on an exit strategy usually within three to seven years (and sometimes longer). Therefore, when selling to a private equity firm, you want to emphasize your company's near-term growth potential, the opportunities for a successful exit and the likelihood that it can be achieved;

• further to the previous point, strategic buyers look to integrate their acquisitions with their existing operations, thereby realizing operating synergies. By contrast, private equity firms will look at your company as an investment within their portfolio. They may not be able to achieve meaningful operating synergies unless they have other portfolio companies that they can combine (which can be the case with "bolt-on" type investments). Consequently, private equity firms will look at the value of your company on an intrinsic basis. However, they may be willing to pay some level of premium if they believe that your company represents an attractive platform opportunity within a desirable industry segment;

- in most cases, strategic buyers prefer to own 100% of their subsidiaries so as to avoid potential issues and the additional accountability stemming from having minority shareholders. Conversely, private equity firms typically prefer where key management individuals invest in the company in order to solidify their commitment. In addition, private equity firms usually prefer that the existing shareholders reinvest some of the sale proceeds into their company, particularly those that were actively involved. This also helps in solidifying commitment and reduces perceived *transition risk*;

- in an effort to gain synergies, many strategic buyers will terminate senior management individuals as part of the acquisition process. By contrast, private equity firms typically look to engage key senior management individuals and entice them to invest in the company in order to secure their commitment; and

- while the amount of debt used to finance an acquisition varies, private equity firms typically use higher amounts of debt financing, sometimes significantly higher, compared to strategic buyers. Of particular note, during the 2006 to mid-2008 era, where debt financing was both inexpensive and readily available, many private equity firms used excessive amounts of debt to finance their acquisitions. These highly leveraged buyouts allowed private equity firms to offer prices for acquisition targets that rivalled those offered by strategic buyers. However, in many cases, the use of excessive leverage backfired where the investee companies were not able to service that debt, particularly in light of tightening credit market conditions in the latter part of 2008. In other words, many private equity firms did not appreciate the level of *financial risk* that they were taking on.

Exhibit 15C : Strategic Buyers vs. Private Equity Firms

Strategic Buyers	Private Equity Firms
Long-term focus	Near-term focus
Integration focus	Portfolio investment focus
Prefer 100% ownership	Prefer that management and existing shareholders have an equity interest
May terminate existing management	Engages existing management
Low to modest amounts of debt financing	Significant debt financing

As noted above, many private equity firms prefer that the existing shareholders retain a residual equity interest in their company in order to solidify their commitment to a smooth transition and to work on growth initiatives. Where this is the case, you should ensure that the private equity firm that you select as a partner is not only offering an attractive price, but that they will help your company to grow and prosper by offering good strategic advice, best practices, sales leads, additional capital to support growth and other benefits. These things can offer existing shareholders the chance to enjoy more potential gain.

However, caution is warranted. Since existing shareholders will hold a minority equity position, they will not be in a position to dictate the timing of the subsequent exit strategy or the realization of value from their residual equity interest. As stated before, any dollar not received at the closing of a transaction represents a dollar at risk, and you have to be satisfied that the potential reward is worth the risk. The provisions of the shareholders' agreement are also important to consider, particularly with respect to decision making, liquidity and valuation.

Therefore, you should view the alternatives for selling your company as a trade-off between (i) maximizing value today by selling to a strategic buyer vs. (ii) receiving some value today from a financial buyer, with potential gain upon the sale of your residual interest at a later date.

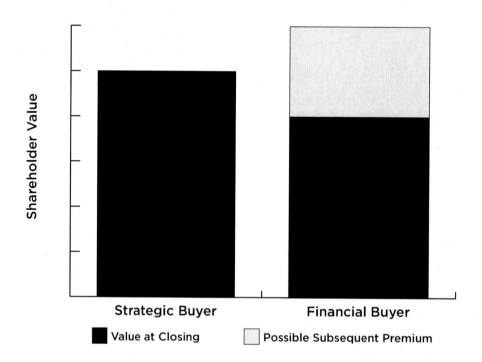

Exhibit 15D : Financial Buyer Tradeoff

Key Points to Remember

- Private equity firms look for companies with strong business fundamentals, a solid management team and an attractive exit strategy.

- The three economic drivers for private equity firms are growth (organic or through acquisition), financial leverage and exit multiple expansion.

- Private equity firms usually prefer where the management team invests in the company and/or existing shareholders retain a residual equity interest.

- Strategic buyers may offer a better price at closing, but a private equity firm can offer existing shareholders and management the opportunity to participate in potential gain.

- Private equity firms can act as a strategic buyer where they already have a portfolio investment in an industry segment.

16 Management Buyouts

A management buyout (MBO) refers to the process of management acquiring a majority or significant minority stake in your company, generally as a means of providing an exit strategy for the existing shareholders. MBOs are also commonly used where a corporation is looking to spin off one or more of its operating divisions.

MBOs can provide a viable exit strategy alternative for business owners and an attractive opportunity for management, particularly if your company has good growth potential and financing can be secured. The financial payoffs from an MBO can be substantial where forecasted operating results and exit strategy expectations are realized.

In most cases where the company or operating division is of a meaningful size, MBOs involve one or more commercial lenders and/or private equity firms who provide financing to facilitate the transaction. The amount of financing required, and whether debt or equity financing is raised, depends on the size of the transaction, the financial resources available to management and the debt capacity of the company.

In this chapter, we'll examine how MBOs work, the financial payoffs and the potential pitfalls.

The MBO Process

MBOs can be thought of as comprising eight stages, which are set out below. However, it should be noted that these stages are not always distinct, and they may overlap or even change order, depending on the deal.

Exhibit 16A : The MBO Process

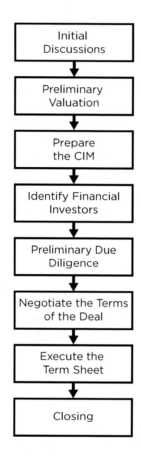

```
┌─────────────────┐
│     Initial     │
│   Discussions   │
└─────────────────┘
          │
          ▼
┌─────────────────┐
│   Preliminary   │
│    Valuation    │
└─────────────────┘
          │
          ▼
┌─────────────────┐
│     Prepare     │
│     the CIM     │
└─────────────────┘
          │
          ▼
┌─────────────────┐
│ Identify Financial │
│    Investors    │
└─────────────────┘
          │
          ▼
┌─────────────────┐
│ Preliminary Due │
│    Diligence    │
└─────────────────┘
          │
          ▼
┌─────────────────┐
│ Negotiate the Terms │
│   of the Deal   │
└─────────────────┘
          │
          ▼
┌─────────────────┐
│   Execute the   │
│   Term Sheet    │
└─────────────────┘
          │
          ▼
┌─────────────────┐
│     Closing     │
└─────────────────┘
```

Initial Discussions

Existing shareholders may approach management, or vice versa, to determine their level of interest in acquiring the company or division. In some cases, management approaches the existing shareholders after the process has begun to sell to a strategic buyer. This can be problematic due to the conflict of interest that it can create. Management may want to downplay the value of your company to strategic buyers in favour of enhancing their own position. In order to avoid such a situation, the existing shareholders will sometimes offer management the opportunity to share in the upside that a strategic buyer will pay, in excess of what management has offered for your company. While this erodes the proceeds received by existing shareholders, it can help to ensure that everyone's interests are aligned.

Preliminary Valuation

The existing shareholders and management should establish a reasonable estimate for the value of your company and how the price will be paid. Negotiating the price and terms for an MBO can be awkward. Unlike negotiations with a strategic buyer, in an MBO the existing shareholders and management already know each other well, and so personal interaction and past experience become a factor. In addition, management has the advantage of first-hand knowledge of your company, including its risk profile and growth prospects. This situation is particularly acute where the existing shareholders were not active in your company prior to the sale and so management has more current and more in-depth information. Management may attempt to downplay your company's strengths and emphasize its risks in order to negotiate a better deal. It's generally good business practice for the parties to jointly retain an independent valuator to help establish a fair price.

Whether or not the preliminary valuation represents the ultimate purchase price will be subject to management's ability to raise capital and the dynamics of negotiations with private equity firms (where they are involved). However, the preliminary valuation exercise helps to ensure that the parties are reasonably aligned with respect to expectations prior to soliciting investor interest.

Preparing the Confidential Information Memorandum (CIM)

Where financial investors (debt or equity) will be required in order to facilitate an MBO, management will need to prepare a confidential information memorandum (CIM) to entice those groups. The CIM should contain sufficient information about your company, its product and service offerings, customer base, market position and financial results to allow prospective investors to assess their level of interest. In particular, the CIM should highlight management's capabilities, strategic plans and growth opportunities, which are key considerations for any investor. The CIM should also include an overview of the proposed transaction structure and terms (e.g., amount of financing sought, minority vs. majority equity position available, etc.).

Unlike a CIM designed to attract a strategic buyer (discussed in the next chapter), a CIM in the context of an MBO should highlight your company's ability to proper as a stand-alone entity (or in conjunction with bolt-on acquisitions). The CIM should also address exit strategy opportunities, which are important to private equity participants.

Identifying Financial Investors

Where external financing is needed to consummate the transaction, the existing shareholders, management and their advisors will identify providers of debt and/or equity financing that may be interested in the deal. Financial investors can generally be categorized as senior debt lenders, mezzanine debt lenders and private equity firms. Senior debt is attractive due to the lower cost of (tax-deductible) interest payments. However, you need to remember that it's not just the cost of financing that needs to be considered, but also the operating restrictions and banking covenants that may be imposed on your company as a condition of financing.

Where the financing gap can be satisfied by debt, that route usually is chosen as it does not result in any equity erosion for management or the existing shareholders who retain a residual interest. However, equity financing may be required where adequate debt financing cannot be secured on reasonable terms. In either case, the existing shareholders and management should endeavor to develop several good financing alternatives in order to create an auction among prospective financial investors.

Preliminary Due Diligence

Financial investors that express an interest in the opportunity are provided a copy of the CIM. Those with a continuing interest following their review of the CIM will conduct further due diligence, including meetings with management and access to additional information (usually provided through an online data room). In this regard, it's important to remember that meetings with financial investors should be viewed as a two-way street. Management and the existing shareholders should strive to learn about the financial investors in terms of the reasons for their interest, relevant experience, operating style and decision-making process. This will not only help in selecting the right financial partners, but such information is essential in negotiating the financing terms.

Negotiating the Terms of the Deal

While the value of your company may be initially negotiated between the existing shareholders and the management team at the outset of the MBO process, it will be subject to the dynamics of further negotiations with lenders and private equity firms (where they are involved). Negotiations are a critical component of the deal and both the existing shareholders and the management team need to understand their alternatives in order to objectively assess their negotiating position and the negotiating strategies they should use.

As with any transaction, the terms of the deal can be just as important as the stated purchase price. In the context of an MBO, some of the particular deal structuring considerations that often arise include the following:

- whether the existing shareholders intend to sell 100% of the company or retain a residual interest. An MBO transaction often is facilitated where the existing shareholders agree to retain a residual interest because it reduces the initial cash outlay required and often provides added comfort for financial investors that the current owners continue to believe in their company. Properly structured, a residual interest can also provide significant potential gain for existing shareholders. They must be cautious, however, as retaining a residual interest means that the existing shareholders will become minority shareholders in their company. Consequently, the terms of a shareholders' agreement become paramount. In particular, the provisions governing decision making, liquidity and valuation of the residual equity interest must be carefully considered;

- promissory notes are common in MBOs, particularly where sufficient commercial debt financing cannot be raised. However, the existing shareholders must be cautious because, unlike strategic buyers that may have other assets to secure the note, management often has minimal security to offer. While the assets of your company can serve as security, the value of those assets can diminish rapidly if your company is mismanaged or unforeseen events occur following the transaction;

- earnout arrangements can be a useful deal structuring tool. Earnouts sometimes are easier for existing shareholders to accept in an MBO situation where they are comfortable with the capabilities and integrity of the management team. Further, there is less concern about the potential impact of changes to your company's operations than there would be with a strategic buyer, who may enact changes that will materially affect your company's financial performance post-closing. However, earnouts are still problematic and represent risk capital for the sellers; and

- the role that the existing shareholders will play after the MBO transaction takes effect. Shareholders who were active in the company should expect to remain active for a period of time following the transaction in order to ensure a smooth transition with employees, customers and suppliers. This transitional assistance may be of particular importance to financial investors.

The Term Sheet

Financial investors that are interested in the opportunity following their preliminary due diligence will submit a term sheet (similar to a letter of intent), which sets out the terms of financing the transaction. In this regard, it's common for financial investors to seek "arrangement fees", "stamping fees" and the recovery of legal costs in order to proceed with the transaction, which can be significant.

The financial investor(s) offering the term sheet that best meets the needs of the existing shareholders and management are provided a period of time to complete their due diligence and to negotiate the definitive agreements.

Closing

The closing of the transaction involves the financial investor's detailed due diligence (e.g., audit, legal, environmental), negotiating the lending agreement (in the case of senior debt and mezzanine lenders), the purchase and sale agreement and related shareholders' agreement (where required) and, finally, closing. The existing shareholders should endeavour to ensure that no surprises arise during the closing period which could jeopardize the deal.

Private Equity Firms and MBOs

When searching for the right private equity partner (where one is required), management will begin by searching for those firms that have stated investment criteria that meet the profile of the company. This includes investment size, industry segment, life cycle stage, geographic location and whether the private equity firm desires a controlling or minority position. These elements were covered in Chapter 11. Also recall from the previous chapter that private equity firms are looking for companies that offer:

- strong business fundamentals, with a defendable niche or sustainable competitive advantage;

- excellent growth potential, either organically or through acquisition;

- a strong management team with a proven track record; and

- exit strategy potential, generally within a three-year to seven-year time frame.

Therefore, the existing shareholders and management team should seek to establish the following prior to soliciting a private equity firm:

- the strategic plan for your company, including opportunities for both organic growth and possible acquisition targets;

- the exit strategy, both in terms of timing and likely buyers;

- the amount of capital that management has available to invest, and the amount that the existing shareholders are willing to leave in the company;

- the expected level of involvement that the existing shareholders will have following the transaction; and

- whether the private equity firm will have a controlling interest or a minority interest.

These parameters will help the existing shareholders and the management team in focusing their efforts on identifying the right private equity partner.

In the context of an MBO, private equity firms will consider the amount of debt that can be placed into your company as part of the transaction. The use of debt allows the private equity firm to reduce the size of their equity investment and magnify their returns. However, it's important to remember that using a lot of debt financing significantly increases your company's financial risk, and may result in cumbersome operating restrictions.

A common misconception among managers is that they will be given shares in the company as part of the transaction on account of their past "sweat equity". But this is usually not the case. Private equity firms generally insist that key managers personally invest in the company in order to have "skin in the game". In most cases, the absolute amount of the investment is not an issue, so long as it represents a meaningful commitment by the individual(s). Managers that do invest can realize lucrative upside potential where things turn out as planned.

Where a private equity firm becomes involved, the MBO process becomes a dynamic discussion among three parties:
  (i)   the existing shareholders seeking to realize on their investment;
  (ii) the management team looking to acquire an equity interest; and
  (iii) the private equity firm seeking a return on invested capital.

The interests of the various parties involved in an MBO are naturally conflicting to some degree. The existing shareholders want the highest price for their company, management wants the ability to acquire the largest equity stake possible in the company, and the private equity firm is seeking to maximize their own return on invested capital. For an MBO to be successful, all parties must make compromises and structure a deal that creates a three-way beneficial scenario. In order to do so, it's critical to engage a facilitator to assist in bringing the parties together.

The facilitator normally is a financial advisor (supported by other consultants, such as legal and tax advisors) who not only understands the workings of an MBO, but who also can offer the parties objective advice on the pros and cons of various alternatives. The principal role of the facilitator is to assist both the existing shareholders and the management team in identifying and attracting the right financial investor "partners" (debt and equity), and in helping to negotiate the terms of a deal that satisfy the collective interests of all parties. In doing so, the facilitator helps the various parties to identify ways in which they can reconcile their respective positions and preserve a sense of "value fairness" to each. The role of the facilitator within the MBO process is captured in the *MBO Value Matrix* [TM], illustrated below.

Exhibit 16B : The MBO Value Matrix™

It's important for both the existing shareholders and the management team to select a private equity firm "partner" that will not only offer an attractive purchase price, but is also aligned in terms of their interests and expectations. Value-added service offerings are important to consider as well, in terms of follow-on financing, strategic advice, industry contacts and so on.

The private equity firm will look closely at the management team, in terms of their abilities, depth (i.e., diversification and succession) and their commitment (including their personal investment in the company). The private equity firm will also gauge their level of interest based on your company's growth potential, debt capacity and exit strategy opportunities.

MBO transactions involving private equity firms are more likely to occur where the existing shareholders have realistic expectations as to the value of their company and they are prepared to work with the management team and the private equity firm in terms of deal structuring and transitional assistance.

How Does an MBO Work?

To illustrate the payoffs involved in an MBO, let's return to our example of Tasty Snacks Ltd. Recall from Chapter 15 that a private equity firm is looking to buy the company for $50 million using $25 million in debt and $25 million in equity. Let's assume that the management team is looking to participate in the deal, and that collectively management can raise $2.5 million. Also assume that the private equity firm wants the current owner (Mr. Goody) to "roll over" $2.5 million of the equity that he receives on the sale of Tasty Snacks, in order to ensure his continued commitment. This can usually be accomplished on a tax-efficient basis. Further, in order to provide an incentive for the management team, the private equity firm decides to offer them potential gain in the form of an ESOP (employee share ownership plan), whereby they can earn an additional 5% equity interest upon achieving certain financial objectives.

Based on the expectations that Tasty Snacks would grow its EBITDA to $13.3 million over the next three years and be sold for a multiple of 6x EBITDA at that time, the financial payoff to the various parties would be as follows:

Exhibit 16C : Management Buyout of Tasty Snacks Ltd. $(000)

	Current Year		Forecast Year 1	Year 2	Year 3	
EBITDA	10,000		11,000	12,100	13,300	
Multiple	5x				6x	
Enterprise Value	50,000				79,800	
Capital Structure						
Opening debt balance	15,000		25,000	27,860	25,121	
Debt additions (repayments)	10,000		2,860	(2,739)	(3,652)	
Total debt	25,000		27,860	25,121	21,469	
Equity	25,000				58,331	

	$	%		$	%
Equity Composition					
Private Equity Firm	20,000	80%		44,072	75.6%
Existing Shareholder	2,500	10%		5,509	9.4%
Management Team	2,500	10%	(Plus ESOP of 5%)	8,750	15.0%
	25,000	100%		58,331	100.0%

Return on Equity		
Private Equity Firm		30%
Existing Shareholder		30%
Management Team		52%
Combined		33%

Note how the initial equity structure is comprised of an 80% ownership interest by the private equity firm, and 10% ownership by each of the existing shareholder (Mr. Goody) and the management team. However, upon the subsequent sale of the company, the management team's interest has increased to 15%, which provides them with the greatest return on equity of 52%. While the ESOP dilutes the ownership interest and the economic returns of the private equity firm, it helps to solidify the commitment of key management individuals. Consequently, the private equity firm is exposed to less risk. MBOs are commonly designed to offer management the greatest investment return, which makes them appealing. This feature drives management's behaviour both before and after the initial transaction. As noted above, this management incentive can become problematic because it creates a conflict of interest and makes it more difficult where existing shareholders are also looking to entice strategic buyers.

Mr. Goody experiences the same pro rata erosion from the ESOP as the private equity firm. However, he gets treated on an equal basis. The benefit to Mr. Goody is that his $2.5 million investment now represents a 10% interest in Tasty Snacks. Prior to the transaction, the equity value of Tasty Snacks was $35 million because it used less debt, which meant that a $2.5

million equity interest only represented about 7%. In effect, Mr. Goody will benefit from the increased financial leverage that was used to acquire Tasty Snacks. Of course, his investment is also exposed to higher financial risk.

Common Obstacles to an MBO Transaction

Despite the potential attractiveness of an MBO, you should also weigh the challenges in consummating the transaction and realizing value in any residual equity interest component. The challenges in consummating the MBO transaction itself include:

- the conflict of interest that it creates for the management team, who want a lower valuation in order to get a bigger equity stake in the company for their investment. Management's conflict of interest can also thwart opportunities with strategic buyers;

- getting key managers to commit capital. Managers may not have the same entrepreneurial spirit as the existing shareholders, and they may be reluctant to commit capital, or have limited ability to do so. Financial investors may be wary of making a significant investment where key employees have not made a meaningful monetary commitment;

- management does not have the ability to realize synergies, unlike a strategic buyer. This can reduce the purchase price. The value impact is somewhat less where a private equity firm which owns a similar business in their portfolio is involved, and can integrate the operations of the two entities; and

- financial investors generally prefer MBOs where the existing shareholders retain a residual interest and remain active in the company following the transaction. This may not be consistent with their objectives. Further, where the existing shareholders do retain a residual equity interest, there is no assurance as to when, or whether, value from that residual interest will be realized. Not only is the nature and timing of the exit strategy outside of their control, but there is the risk of changes in the company's performance, industry conditions or the collapse of potential liquidity events (due to a weakening mergers and acquisitions market), that can significantly erode shareholder value during the interim period.

Following the MBO transaction, there will be further challenges in having a private equity firm as a partner, which include their focus on short term results, additional governance and reporting requirements and the increased risks and covenants where your company is exposed to higher levels of debt financing. These issues were addressed in Chapter 11.

Key Points to Remember

- Be aware of the conflict of interest that MBOs create for management.

- Injecting additional debt in your company to finance an MBO will leverage share-holder returns but also increase financial risk.

- When selecting the right financial investor(s), consider their ability to be a good business partner as well as the amount of capital they are willing to invest.

- MBOs require that management be prepared to invest a meaningful amount of cash for their shares and not just rely on "sweat equity".

- Private equity firms will not invest in a company where they cannot foresee an attractive exit strategy within their intended investment horizon.

17 Selling to Strategic Buyers

For a business owner, the sale of their company can be the single largest financial event of their lifetime. What's more, it's as much an emotional decision as it is an economic decision. While a divestiture is less personal for directors and executives of a public company, the sale process can none the less be an emotional roller coaster.

A large part of my professional life has been spent helping business owners and executives to sell their company. Each situation has been unique. I was well into my career as a mergers and acquisitions (M&A) advisor before I discovered that all of the economic "voodoo" that can be practised with respect to financial models is only part of the process. So much depends on psychology, deal structuring and negotiation, including the need and the desire of the buyer and the seller to transact.

This chapter will provide an overview of the sale process and some of the key elements and strategies that business owners and executives should consider. If you are keenly interested in learning more about this topic, I suggest that you read another book that I wrote, *"Selling Your Private Company: The Value Enhancement Framework™ for Business Owners"*, also published by the Canadian Institute of Chartered Accountants (2005).

The Sale Process

In *Selling Your Private Company*, the sale process is divided into eight distinct steps:

1. deciding when to sell;

2. preparing your company for sale;

3. preliminary valuation;

4. searching for buyers;

5. preliminary due diligence;

6. deal structuring;

7. negotiations; and

8. closing.

The first three steps represent the *planning phase*, which occurs prior to the time your company is exposed to the market. Appropriate planning can take years to complete, but it's essential in order to set the foundation for the sale process.

The next five steps are the *execution phase*, during which time the seller is approaching and negotiating with buyers in order to get the best deal possible. The key to maximizing shareholder value in this part of the process is to create an effective auction for your company. A well-executed auction with the right buyers will serve to build shareholder value throughout the sale process.

Exhibit 17A : The Sale Process

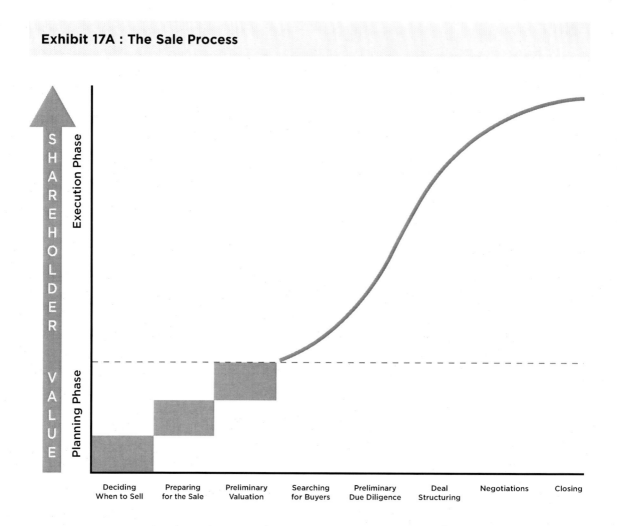

Planning for the Sale

Deciding When to Sell

The first question that most business owners ask is "when is a good time to sell my company?" There is no magic formula that can be used to determine this. However, timing is usually best when industry and economic conditions are relatively strong (hence creating more liquidity in the market) *and* your company is an attractive acquisition target because of its financial performance and competitive advantage. In this regard, buyers tend to have a greater level of interest in companies that have demonstrated growth in both revenues and cash flow *and* where growth is expected to continue.

Exhibit 17B illustrates this point. Selling at a point where financial performance has been soft, and relying on the "great potential" of your company usually means receiving less value, as most buyers will not pay for speculation (at least not in the form of cash on closing). At the other end of the curve is a situation where your company has grown its revenues and cash flows, but future growth is limited. This will negatively influence the valuation multiple. Remember that the enterprise value of your company is a function of its expected cash flows and the valuation multiple. The product of these two variables usually is maximized around the middle of the curve, at a point where your company has demonstrated success and growth is likely to continue (as evidenced by new customers, new product and service offerings, etc.).

Exhibit 17B : Timing the Sale of Your Company

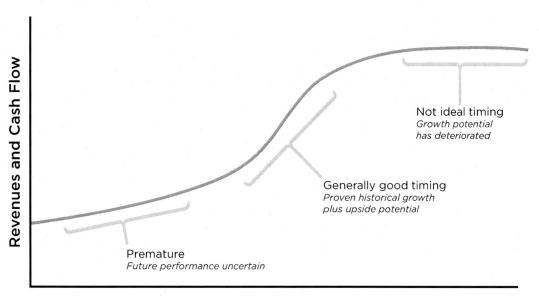

Revenues and Cash Flow

Not ideal timing
*Growth potential
has deteriorated*

Generally good timing
*Proven historical growth
plus upside potential*

Premature
Future performance uncertain

Time

Preparing Your Company for Sale

You only get one chance to make a first impression. Remember that many buyers, particularly large, well-financed companies, are inundated with solicitations from would-be sellers. The executives at those companies have to select which opportunities best meet their acquisition criteria and provide the greatest potential for gain. Therefore, you need to position your company as an attractive acquisition opportunity from the start.

So ask yourself: "Why would someone want to buy my company?" It usually has more to do with the competitive advantage and intangible value that your company has to offer than its physical assets. Buyers are interested in the unique attributes of your company's product and service offerings, its customer base and the strength of its management team. These are the same factors that lead to a higher valuation multiple, which were discussed in Chapter 2. It follows that *the initiatives that you should undertake prior to selling your company are those that are conducive to building a competitive advantage.* Remember that buyers will assess the *transition risk* associated with your company – that is, the degree to which your company's competitive advantage may not be sustainable or transferable. So you need to demonstrate that things like "customer stickiness" and management succession plans do exist.

In many cases, there is a tremendous opportunity to realize shareholder value before your company is exposed for sale in the open market. For example, there may be excess working capital on your balance sheet, which is easier to extract prior to contacting prospective buyers than after the sale process has begun. Remember, it's not the best price, but the best deal that you should be focused on attaining.

Pre-sale planning goes beyond your company itself. There are three parties to every deal – the buyer, the seller and the government. In many cases, there are opportunities to reduce the government's piece by legitimately reducing or deferring the income taxes payable on a transaction, in which case both the buyer and the seller could end up being winners. However, tax and estate planning often take time to prepare and implement, so starting well ahead of time is key.

This is also the time to engage the right professionals to assist you in the divestiture, including legal counsel, tax advisors and M&A advisors. You should ensure that the professionals you engage have both the expertise and experience to navigate you through the sale process, and that they can advise you in an objective manner. The role of the intermediary should be to develop quality alternatives and to provide you with the information that you need to make an informed decision which satisfies both your financial and personal interests.

Initial Valuation

It's a good idea to engage a firm that will provide an objective assessment of your company's value before the sale process begins. This will help to ensure that your expectations with respect to value are realistic. The valuation process should include an analysis of industry transactions, which may help in identifying possible buyers.

Properly conducted, a pre-sale valuation will also help in terms of identifying initiatives that can make your company a more attractive acquisition target prior to soliciting buyers and other value enhancement initiatives.

Executing the Sale

Finding Buyers

The key to creating an effective auction begins by attracting a sufficient number of qualified buyers who have the interest and the ability to consummate a transaction on terms that you find acceptable. In this regard, extensive research is key to understanding who might be a qualified buyer and why. You should consider companies within your industry that have been involved in recent transactions, and publicly listed companies that have a stated interest in growing through acquisition.

While direct competitors may be logical buyers, you should also consider companies in other industry segments that would benefit from having access to your company's competitive advantage. *The ideal buyer is one that views your company as a platform for growth due to their ability to leverage your company's product and service offerings, its customer base and employees.* Platform buyers focus on synergies in the form of incremental revenues, and are more likely to pay for that benefit, as contrasted with buyers who focus solely on cost reduction.

Of course, don't forget about private equity firms, as discussed in Chapter 15. Private equity firms can sometimes be categorized as strategic buyers where they have other investments in their portfolio that allow them to realize synergies and, in particular, where the private equity firm is pursuing a consolidation or "roll-up" strategy.

Qualified buyers should sign a confidentiality agreement or non-disclosure agreement (NDA). However, you should recognize that an NDA only affords a limited amount of protection. A breach of confidentiality is difficult to prove and costly to enforce. Therefore, it's important for you to remain in control of the information dissemination process to ensure that sensitive information is not disclosed prematurely, particularly when dealing with industry participants and direct competitors.

Maintaining confidentiality is always a concern in the sale process. Employees that learn of the impending sale may become concerned about job security. In some cases, it may be wise to take certain key employees into confidence about the sale process and assure them that their interests will be protected in exchange for their commitment to the company. While there may be a cost in doing so (e.g., pay-to-stay bonuses), the loss of key employees can be detrimental to receiving an attractive offer.

Preliminary Due Diligence

Preliminary due diligence refers to the process of providing information about your company to prospective buyers. This is done through a confidential information memorandum (CIM), meetings with prospective buyers and allowing buyers access to a data room (typically online).

The CIM should provide a meaningful overview of your company so that prospective buyers can establish whether it represents a strategic fit for them. The CIM contains information about the operations of your company, its history, product and service offerings, customer base and limited financial data (such as gross sales and normalized EBITDA). As the first piece of non-public information that the buyer will review, the CIM should be designed to convey your company as an attractive acquisition candidate and to motivate prospective buyers to move relatively quickly to seize that opportunity. However, it should not contain detailed or highly sensitive information.

Buyers that remain interested in your company are invited to meet with you and members of your company's management team that are privy to the sale. The protocol for initial buyer meetings should be established beforehand to ensure that the focus of such meetings remains on determining whether there is a fit between your company and the buyer, as opposed to discussing the price and terms of a deal at this point. It's customary to prepare a management presentation to elaborate on the information provided in the CIM. At this meeting you should ask questions about the buyer's operations and the reasons for their interest in your company, which can prove useful in subsequent negotiations.

Qualified buyers who continue to express an interest are then provided access to a secure data room containing additional information about your company. The information contained in the data room normally includes more details on your company's historical financial performance, projections, customers, suppliers, operations and so on, which should be sufficient to allow the buyer to prepare a meaningful letter of intent (LOI).

It's important that you control the information dissemination process, not only to protect against premature disclosure of sensitive information, but also to help in escalating the auction process. However, it's also important to ensure that all material factors affecting your company (both positive and negative) are disclosed prior to executing an LOI with a particular buyer. Attempting to hide significant information can be detrimental to the sale process where it is subsequently uncovered by the buyer. At that point, your negotiating position is diminished and the transaction may not proceed, or the terms of sale may be far less favourable.

Deal Structuring

The structure of the deal has a significant impact on the price that may (or may not) ultimately be received, and the resultant income tax consequences. As a result, the terms of the deal are just as important as the stated purchase price. In other words, the highest price offered for your company may not represent the best deal. Maximizing shareholder value rests in structuring a deal with acceptable risk-reward parameters in a tax-efficient manner.

Recall from the discussion in Chapter 12 that deal structuring involves three major elements:

• whether you sell the assets or the shares of your company;

• the forms of consideration; and

• the management contract.

As a general rule, buyers prefer to buy the underlying assets of a company as it provides them with certain income tax advantages and reduces the risk of assuming hidden liabilities. However, there are tax advantages to the seller when shares are sold. A share sale can also simplify the transfer of contracts and other legal rights to the buyer. Therefore, the question of assets vs. shares usually comes down to assessing the after-tax proceeds that will be realized under each alternative.

The terms of payment dictate when, how, and under what conditions the purchase price will (or will not) be paid. Most sellers prefer to receive 100% cash on closing. However, this seldom is the case in the sale of a private company. Other common forms of consideration include holdbacks, promissory notes, share exchanges and earnout arrangements, which were discussed in Chapter 12.

Remember that any portion of the purchase price that is not received in the form of cash on the closing of the transaction is subject to risk of non-payment. Therefore, you should be satisfied that the potential reward offsets the risk that is taken. You should also consider the tax implications of non-cash forms of consideration. If you are not careful, you could end up paying tax before receiving the sale proceeds. Professional advice is usually warranted in this regard.

Where you were actively involved in your company prior to the sale, the buyer will usually want you to enter into some form of management or consulting contract, in order to help ensure a smooth transition. Buyers will also require that you enter into a non-competition agreement, which defines the nature, duration and geographic scope of activities that you are prohibited from engaging in following the sale. You must be satisfied that such restrictions will not unduly affect your plans or lifestyle following the sale.

Negotiations

Business owners and executives sometimes fail to recognize the importance of negotiations when selling their company. The key elements in effectively negotiating the sale on attractive terms rest in your ability to do the following:

- **gather information.** The more that you understand why a buyer is interested in your company and the synergies that they will realize, the better able you are to position your company as an attractive acquisition candidate;

- **establish and retain credibility.** This means that you should not make statements that cannot be supported. For example, if you overestimate your company's near-term financial performance in order to entice buyers, there will be a credibility issue when those results do not materialize;

- **maintain flexibility,** which refers to understanding the costs and benefits of various deal structures and whether those deal structures satisfy your personal and financial objectives. Remember that the structure of the deal is just as important as the stated purchase price; and

- **develop meaningful alternatives.** Negotiating strategy is a function of the number and quality of interested buyers and the offers made for your company. In this regard, you should consider all of the ways that shareholder value can be realized, including through ongoing dividends, management buyouts and other avenues.

Interested buyers will prepare an LOI, setting out the proposed terms of the deal. You should carefully consider the content of an LOI received from a prospective buyer prior to agreeing to same. When you countersign the LOI, it grants the buyer a period of exclusivity (normally 60 to 120 days) to complete their due diligence and negotiate a definitive agreement of purchase and sale. While not legally binding (except for certain provisions, such as exclusivity), the LOI sets the stage for the balance of the sale process and provides a framework for the purchase and sale agreement. Shareholder value is maximized where an effective auction is created so that all prospective buyers submit LOI's around the same time, which allows you to negotiate with buyers in competition with each other.

A shrewd buyer will try to get you to agree to exclusivity early on, but you generally should resist this temptation. The key is to ensure that any LOI received from a buyer is comprehensive in that it should address all significant elements of the deal in a clear and unambiguous manner. Any aspects of the deal that are not clearly established in the LOI are subject to negotiation during the exclusivity period. At that time, your alternatives are limited (because you cannot readily engage another buyer) and therefore your negotiating position is weaker.

Closing the Deal

The closing of the deal involves the buyer's detailed due diligence, the finalization of the purchase and sale agreement and the closing itself. During the course of detailed due diligence, the buyer will carefully examine all aspects of your company's financial records, operations, customers, etc., in order to be satisfied that their facts and assumptions about your company are complete and accurate, and that no undisclosed issues exist. In this regard, it's important for you to ensure that any major issues facing your company have been disclosed prior to the LOI being signed in order to avoid a substantial renegotiation of the deal or the deal failing to close.

The purchase and sale agreement, which normally is drafted by the buyer, represents the binding contract to acquire your company. You should strive to ensure that the negotiations of the purchase and sale agreement proceed smoothly by maintaining some degree of flexibility in order to meet the buyer's concerns following their findings in the detailed due diligence phase. You should pay particular attention to the representations and warranties in the purchase and sale agreement that may fundamentally increase the risk to you, and therefore diminish the value effectively received for your company.

The closing of the deal normally takes place concurrently with the signing of the purchase and sale agreement or shortly thereafter. Following the closing date, a final audit will be conducted to verify the financial accounts of your company, which may result in an adjustment to the purchase price (e.g., on account of working capital or other specified target measures). This can represent an opportunity to receive a premium for your company, where these things have been properly planned for and negotiated.

Don't underestimate the amount of time and effort that will be required from you and your management team to go through due diligence and close the deal. Furthermore, it's important for you to remain focused on your company's operations throughout the closing period. Any material erosion in your company's financial or operating performance during the closing period can prove detrimental, as the buyer may seek to renegotiate the price or terms of sale.

Why Deals Fail to Close

There are numerous reasons why a deal may fail to close. Some of these reasons are related to the buyer, such as the inability to raise the required financing or the transaction not being approved by the buyer's Board of Directors. This is why it's important to develop good alternatives.

Another common reason for deals failing to close relates to the LOI. Where the LOI is loosely worded, then the buyer and seller may have wildly differing expectations as to the terms of the deal. A clear, comprehensive LOI is essential in order to avoid this situation.

It can also be problematic where the buyer uncovers something unexpected during its detailed due diligence investigation. One of the golden rules to remember is that there should be *no surprises after the LOI has been signed*.

In some cases, a company's performance deteriorates late in the sale process, such as when it loses a major customer or experiences quality control problems. This can happen where there is too much focus on selling the company and not enough attention is paid to running it. You should ensure that the operations of the company are not compromised during the sale process.

Finally, there is always the risk of external factors disrupting the sale process, such as the credit crisis that erupted in late 2008 which caused financing for acquisitions to quickly evaporate. While these things are beyond your control, you can limit the risk of external factors by keeping the time frame for detailed due diligence as short as possible. Remember that work extends to meet the time allowed for its completion!

Exhibit 17C : Why Deals Fail to Close

- Buyer non-performance
- Ambiguity in the LOI
- Due diligence surprises
- Deteriorating company performance
- External factors

Key Points to Remember

- The best time to sell is when your company has experienced growing revenues and cash flows, and growth is expected to continue.

- The best buyer is one that views your company as a platform for growth because they can realize additional value by leveraging your customers, product and service offerings and employees.

- Control the sale process in order to create an effective auction for your company.

- Secure a comprehensive LOI that sets out all of the key aspects of the deal.

- Focus on getting the best deal for your company, not just the highest price.